SEATED
IN THE CLOUDS,
RULING
ON THE EARTH

DISCOVERING YOUR DUAL POSITION IN CHRIST

A 40-DAY JOURNEY

As always...

Stay Fiery!

APRIL BABB
FOREWORD BY: KATHERINE RUONALA

April Babb

ISBN 978-1-64028-266-7 (Paperback)
ISBN 978-1-64028-268-1 (Hard Cover)
ISBN 978-1-64028-267-4 (Digital)

Christian Faith Publishing, Inc.
296 Chestnut Street
Meadville, PA 16335
www.christianfaithpublishing.com

Printed in the United States of America

Insight from Readers and Friends of the Ministry

"God confirmed many things to me and gave me fresh vision through the words April wrote. I am so thankful for her obedience and unique perspective on the concepts she explored in *Seated in the Clouds, Ruling on the Earth*."

Rebeckah Szmansky, Assistant Prayer Director, Enkindle Ministries
Temperance, MI

"As I started on this journey through *Seated in the Clouds, Ruling on the Earth*, I was so excited, in my spirit, to read what the Lord was revealing. April's obedience was and is an inspiration to me! Her charisma and love for the Lord is contagious. I absolutely loved it!"

Dana Turner, WUCC 99.9 Aiken Radio Host and Deliverance Team Minster,
Aiken, SC

"Attention bride! As you prepare to read this book, be aware that you are starting a journey. Inside the covers of this book you will realize how important you are to God and how much authority He has given you. April leads us on a journey that confirms God's love and trust in us in how He has equipped us for spiritual battle. We are His bride and He wants us to live victorious and to boldly share His love and authority with others. So strap up your boots and put on your armor as we sharpen our swords together. Let's dive into this devotional and get a better understanding of who we are in Christ."

Paul Babb, Founder of People Ablaze Ministry
North Augusta, SC

"April Babb, in one simple word, is LOVE! The love of Jesus shines through her onto everyone she encounters. She has been a beacon of love, hope, and encouragement in my life for many years. As you read the pages of this book, I know you too will feel the warmth of her love, the kindness of her heart, and the hope of Jesus!"
Jenny Davis Hill, April's Prayer Partner
Warrenville, SC

"April has been a beautiful source of godly influence and encouragement to myself and my family. Her excellent knowledge and application of the Word of God has brought great insight. April prays with power and authority and writes with the same. The words written in *Seated in the Clouds* were not only perfectly and prophetically in season but also articulate, loaded with discernment, and clearly speak of the depth of her relationship with her Savior. April beautifully brings Heaven to Earth, preparing a bountiful banquet of truth to feast upon."
Josephine Lake, CEO and Founder, Polka Duck Threads
New South Wales, Australia

"April Babb is a woman of the Word. She keeps her eyes fixed on what the Word (written and rhema) is speaking to the Bride. God gives her fresh insight into His heart and practical ways to apply this wisdom. I am personally amazed that, in addition to growing a ministry with her husband, she also works a nursing job and does an excellent job raising five children to be God-fearing adults."
Jeri Lord Bracey, Member of People Ablaze Bible Study Group
Aiken, SC

"*Seated in the Clouds, Ruling on the Earth* gives such a great picture of our dual spiritual position. April has opened my eyes to an often misunderstood and confusing concept that the Lord desires for us to stand firmly in. I believe that as we allow this revelation to grow in us and solidify in our spirit, we will know how to better recognize the enemy, take authority over him, and live victoriously."
Lynn Sullivan, Content Coordinator/Associate Publisher
Aiken, SC

"The power of the Holy Spirit continues to increase exponentially in the Church of America through miracles, signs, wonders, and healings. After personally ministering alongside April Babb for many years, I have no doubt the supernatural revelation she brings to the Body of Christ has only begun to rouse a divine movement. This writing is divinely inspired to equip His people to pray from a Spirit-led approach, producing significant freedom, and awakening a deep hunger for more of His dynamic power. April's teachings effortlessly catapult the reader to new heights of His glory—all while restfully being 'seated in the clouds' of His Presence."
Christy Austin, Vice President, Enkindle Ministries
Aiken, SC

"April has a way of captivating you as you listen to the voice of God through her words. God has confirmed things to me because of her obedience. I pray for open ears and eyes as you embark on this journey too. Get ready!"
Suzanne Grimaud, Author/Speaker/Business Leader
www.MyChoicessMatter.com
Oklahoma City, OK

"In *Seated in the Clouds, Ruling on the Earth*, the Holy Spirit uses April to give us new spiritual eyes on the authority we carry in Christ. Her charm and perspective keep you encouraged and ready to take on life."
Belinda Gatlin, Prayer Pillar Director, Enkindle Ministries
Amarillo, TX

My *"Keep Going"* Bookmark

Just

One

More

Day . . . .

And God raised us up with Christ and seated us with Him in heavenly realms
—Ephesians 2:6

Then God said, "Let Us make mankind in Our image... so that they may rule over... the Earth."
—Genesis 1:26

Cut out and use to keep up with the reading!

Foreword

What an important and wonderful revelation to meditate on! This beautiful devotional provides us with daily encouragements to remember that we are seated with Christ in heavenly places and anointed to release His authority on earth.

The book of James tells us that we are not to "...merely listen to the word, and so deceive ourselves. We are to do what it says. Anyone who listens to the word but does not do what it says is like someone who looks at his face in a mirror and, after looking at himself, goes away and immediately forgets what he looks like." (James 1:22-24) The Lord wants to remind us daily that as new creations in Christ we now look like Him, for "as He is, so are we in this world" (1 John 4:17). We must believe this if we are to manifest Him on earth and be "doers" of the word.

Rest with your beloved in the place of peace and power as you grow in your understanding of being seated with Him. My prayer is, that through this devotional you will grow more aware of the Father's love for you and the begin to live in the holy confidence He has destined for you.

Katherine Ruonala
Author of "Living in the Miraculous",
"Wilderness to Wonders" and "Life with the Holy Spirit"
www.katherineruonala.com

Acknowledgements

I must offer thanks to God for this amazing journey. I had decided to dedicate this book to Him, but He spoke to me that my life is all He desires and to dedicate the book to the people that helped make it possible! So here goes!

To my best friend and husband, Paul: Your support and consistent allowance to follow my dreams, at all costs, has been selfless and full of love. You've built confidence in me that I once did not have. Thank you.

To Jordan, my eldest: Thank you for letting your mom work on the computer a whole lot and for keeping the little ones fed and entertained on several occasions. You are a duplicate of your father and that makes me very happy.

To the younger members of the Babb tribe: Kylie, Bella, Judah, and Jasper: Mommy loves you and hopes, one day, you'll be as proud of her as she is of you. I love you guys.

To all the supporters of this book and ministry: There are too many of you to name, which makes me smile as well. I've not done this alone and I appreciate God's help that I've received through you all. You are all a part of this book.

To the reader holding this book in their hands: I'm grateful for you, because you're proof that this was the right sacrifice to make. Someone will read this and that makes it worth it all!

About this project

In 2015, while in prayer, the Lord gave me a vision of the words, "Seated in the Clouds, Ruling on the Earth," and the image of a staircase from earth to Heaven that we live on. The only way I can describe it is He began to give me a heavenly download into my spirit of knowledge I had not previously possessed. I began to understand the importance of our dual-position in Heaven with Christ *and* on the earth ruling in His name. He began to pour a passion into me to share this with others; however, I had no platform to do this at the time. A few months later, I began to feel an urgency to start a web site and a blog for our ministry, People Ablaze. The Lord reminded me of the dream in my heart to release the information He had poured in. I launched a web site and a blog that same day! I knew it would be a devotional book, but the Lord led me to release the writings one day at a time. This was so helpful, for a new author, to keep me on task but not make me overwhelmed. It was like eating an elephant one bite at a time, which made it possible for a working mother of five. The best and unexpected benefit of writing this way was the dialogue that occurred between the blog readers and myself. Once the series was completed, I took a break…a much needed one! But then a few months later, I got back to the project, adding ten additional days of testimonies.

This book is "me" on paper. I welcome you into my life to share what God has revealed and blessed me with, and I pray it blesses you as well! Today I submit to you the project, *Seated in the Clouds, Ruling on the Earth*! My passion is to teach the church *who* she is, w*hose* she is, and *where* she is seated! This book is the platform that God has given for me to do just that. The journey you are about to embark on is not for the faint of heart. It is a forty-day expedition into the new you! I believe if you commit time daily to meditate on the words in this devotional, you will be inspired and forever changed as I have been!

April Babb

Monday Back to the Beginning: Adam and Eve

In order for us to take our rightful place in Christ, we must first understand how it all began. God created a world and then put mankind right in the middle of that world to rule. He, in His unlimited power, chose to give dominion, authority, power, and care over the earth into the hands of mankind. And once God does something, it's done! When it came to His creating humanity, He did it differently. He spoke all of creation into being until it came to us. The Word speaks in Genesis 1:26 of the first conversation in recorded history. God had a talk with Himself, and it was about us!

And God said, "Let us make man in our image, after our likeness: and let them have dominion over...all the earth, and over every creeping thing that creepeth upon the earth."

This, my friend, was good news for us all. We will look more into this verse later this week.

There's a principle about God that we learn early in Genesis. Once He gives a gift, He does not take it back. Romans 11:29 reiterates this for us.

The gifts and calling of God are without repentance.

Whether Adam handled it well or poorly, this dominion was his to wield. Authority over the earth was given to Adam both as a gift and a calling. With it came a blessing *and* a responsibility. Of course, we know the tragic story that follows. The one boundary God had set was crossed. It is impossible to be a free agent without the ability to rebel. This sounds strange, but think about it. Those without choice are slaves. God wanted sons! God, out of His love for us, gave us the power of choice, and sadly, humanity chose wrong.

The effect of this one tiny bite began a ripple effect that would only grow in magnitude. Sin had entered, dominion had been forfeited freely to the enemy, and the communion with the Creator was cut off. The enemy hasn't changed his game plan. This week we will focus on our lives and how our enemy desires to strip us of our God-given authority in many ways. May the act of Adam and Eve be in the forefront of our minds this week reminding us, crying out to us, "Run from the fruit. It looks good, but it is toxic!" May the story of Genesis preach a cautionary warning to stay close to the Lord and to shun sin.

Father God, Creator, we recognize that You gave humanity control over the earthly realm. We thank You for the awesome privilege of ruling with Christ Jesus. May we remember and learn from the first of our kind. May their compromise to trade their authority for a tasty indulgence ring in our ears. Each time we lean toward sin and away from the You, may we hear the crunch of the fruit! Help us to be strengthened by Your Word to rise above rebellion. We pledge our love and devotion to You today. We choose obedience. Cleanse us of our sin by Your blood this day! In Jesus' name, we pray. Amen.

Tueday Back to the Beginning: Adam and Eve

As we previously discussed, the Lord's original plan for mankind was dominion and authority over the earth. That plan was usurped by humanity when Adam handed his authority over to Satan. Although one bite of fruit would not seem significant in the physical, in the spiritual it was an atomic bomb going off, only bigger! In Bible study, it is wise to keep thoughts directed to the spiritual significance of any given subject. Everything the Lord does has both physical and spiritual implications. Since we are created in His image, much of what we do affects both realms as well. Today's discussion will parallel the physical and spiritual perspectives of our dominion on the earth.

In Genesis 1:26, God gives humanity dominion over everything earth-bound. He mentions fish, birds, cattle, and *all the Earth* and then comes the latter half of verse 26, which has become one of my favorite statements in the Bible! "Let them have dominion over…every creeping thing that *creepeth* upon the Earth." Don't miss this! God had already given dominion over *all the Earth* and then inserts this statement about creeping things. When you pull out your *Strong's Concordance* and search *Creeping thing*, the most amazing revelation comes, or at least it did for me! Creeping thing comes from the Hebrew word *remes*, which means a reptile or any other rapidly moving animal. Fireworks should already be going off in your head, but let me pound the point further. The word *creepth* itself comes from the Hebrew word *ramas*, which means to glide swiftly, to crawl, or to move with short steps. There is one image that comes to mind when I hear these two definitions: a serpent, also known as a snake![1]

The Lord placed into mankind authority over the enemy at their creation, and the enemy knew it! He still knows it! His attempt is to make us forget it. He uses persuasive words and knows how to camouflage himself into a creeping thing. He didn't come to Eve as a lion or a bear; he came as a small lowly serpent. There was nothing intimidating about an animal a few inches off the ground! Of course, *now* there is a fear of snakes, but that is just one effect from the fall (see Genesis 3:14). Before that, there was no fear of this small creature.

Satan also uses logic. I believe logic and reason are some of his most elusive but powerful weapons. They are often fear and doubt masquerading as concern. Remember the trick he used with Eve in Genesis 3:1?

"Hath God really said?"

Then he began pouring out reason. Oh, that we begin to see through the charade and refuse to give him any authority in our lives. The enemy's main goal, I believe, is to hide, and he does it well however may we enact Ephesians 5:11 and "expose the works of darkness." In Christ, we have been restored to rule over creeping things, aka the Devil and his kingdom! Let's not allow him to fool us into thinking otherwise. It's time to rise up, expose his works, and destroy them through Christ!

Wow, Lord, Your Word is amazing. It is alive and sharp, cutting away deception. You have always intended for us to rule over the enemy and not the other way around. God, we pray to You through Your Son that our eyes will begin to open wider to the enemy and his futile attempts to seize control. We refuse any longer to give an inch to him through sin. Lord, forgive us our sins. We are covered with Your blood and forgiveness. All the authority Jesus purchased as a man, He has given to us. May we not waste it a minute longer. We are utterly in need of Your grace to empower us to keep Satan under our feet. Help us, Holy Spirit. In Jesus' name. Amen.

Wednesday Back to the Beginning: Adam and Eve

Thus far, we have discussed the authority mankind was given at Creation. We know that Adam and Eve forfeited their rule to Satan through disobedience to God. But today we are going to consider what else they lost with that infamous bite of rebellion. As the title indicates, we are studying being "seated in the clouds" and "ruling on the earth." Our focus has been on ruling on the earth through studying our position over the enemy. Today we will reflect on being seated in the clouds by studying our position near the Father. Remember, the condition at creation was God's original intent for humanity. That dual position was dominion over the enemy and closeness to God! The Father's desire for this has not changed. We can return to this place once again!

Mankind was God's crown jewel of Creation. He saved the best for last by creating us in His image and breathing into us His very breath. Oh, the glory of it all as Adam rose from the soil! From the moment Adam first breathed, he lived in intimacy with the Creator. When Adam exhaled, it was God's breath coming out. What a thought that is! After creating Adam, God's next act was to plant a garden. God fashioned a flawless home for Adam, and it suited him perfectly. This garden held more than greenery and water. Within the garden, gifts were placed. The first gift was the location itself, given as an abode of peace for Adam. Secondly, all the provision Adam needed was deposited into the garden.

And out of the ground made the Lord God to grow every tree that is pleasant to the sight, and good for food; the tree of life also in the midst of the garden, and the tree of knowledge of good and evil. And a river went out of Eden to water the garden (Genesis 2:9-10a)

When we are sitting in the clouds with Jesus, aka our Eden, everything we need is present whether it be love, rest, peace, refreshment, healing, provision, restoration, or salvation. It is readily available. *Eden* is the original Hebrew word and translates pleasure, delicate, delight, soft, or to live voluptuously. Isn't that a beautiful word picture of being seated with Christ?

May our reflection bring us back to Eden. I pray we meditate on our access through Christ to be joined with the Father again. Sin has separated us long enough! Satan has separated us long enough! Fear has separated us long enough! All of the blockades have been obliterated through the Cross, the Blood of Jesus, and His Resurrection from the grave.

Speaking of Satan, the thief comes to steal, kill, and destroy according to John 10:10a. But how does he accomplish this mission in our lives? Every weapon he uses purposes to separate us from our place in Christ. He knows the power that position holds for us and wants desperately to keep us from it. However, the latter half of the above verse holds the key to our freedom. It is the one-two punch that decks the enemy every time. When Jesus uttered the below words, truth was dispersed for all eternity.

"I have come that they might have life, and that they might have it more abundantly."

This, my friend, is the gift of Eden in our lives. His presence is our Eden, and life abundant is the gift that is embedded in that presence. This is good news for us. We have been granted access back to the Garden.

Let's go!

Father, we can see through Scripture Your desire for relationship with us. We are humbled that we can sit with Jesus at Your right hand. It is in this place that we can return to Eden. We take Ephesians 2:6 as our anthem! We thank You that You "have raised us up together and made us to sit together in heavenly places in *Christ Jesus" now! Christ Jesus is our* door *to get back to You, Father. May we cease staying at the gate because of fear, sin, or Satan. May we begin to flood into that secret place as we learn that we are meant to be beside You always. We pray all this in Jesus' name! Amen.*

Thursday Back to the Beginning: Adam and Eve

I am intrigued with Adam's story. He was created in God's image, given all authority over the earth, and put in close relationship with God. And he still failed. This speaks to our frailty as humans. We have been awarded all the same benefits as Adam through Jesus. Yet many times we forfeit them just as he did through our sin. However, I do believe there is hope for the church! I believe the day is here that we should embrace our position and privilege of living in Christ and through His Spirit. The Church is coming alive! I feel it, others feel it, the Word prophesied it; His Spirit is being poured out. The latter rain has begun. The time is now for resurrection life to be released!

May we continue to learn from our granddad, Adam. The wise ones learn from others' mistakes so they do not have to repeat them. Let's learn about a few pitfalls Adam fell in so when the same temptations come, we will be ready to stand!

Immediately after the crunch was heard, the Bible paints a vivid picture of an altered Adam. Once carefree and bold in approaching God and walking in authority, he now found himself full of shame. The Bible says, "And *he* did eat. And the eyes of them *both* were opened, and they knew they were naked" (Genesis 3:6b-7).

Disobedience to God will always open our eyes in this way. Did you notice that Eve's eyes were not opened when she ate, but only when Adam did? Remember, he was given authority over all the earth realm. This included her! Authority is a very powerful thing. This act of indulgence did not open their eyes in the way they had hoped for. When we sin, our sin-eyes are opened. What do I mean by this?

Before sin entered, the couple's focus was on God and His love. He was their sole focus. After sin, their attention was fully immersed in themselves, their sin, and their nakedness.

I believe before sin entered they were actually clothed. You're thinking, *April, what do you mean by this? The Bible was clear that they were uncovered and had no shame before sin entered.* The type of clothing I speak of is not the physical kind. Remember, we are being challenged to engage our spiritual eyes during this study and look beyond the surface to the deep truths! I believe they were clothed with the feathers of God. They were under His shadow, under His covering. It reminds me of Psalm 91:1: "He that dwelleth in the secret place of the most High God, shall abide under the shadow of the Almighty." When they sinned, that covering was no longer able to blanket them. God is Holy and cannot intermingle with sin. In that moment when rebellion was birthed, they became and were made aware of their nakedness, physically *and* spiritually.

Their response to their own sin was a mistake we often repeat. They fashioned for themselves a covering of fig leaves to *hide* their sinful state. Don't we do the same thing? At first, the weight of our sin is so heavy it's all we can see. Our sin-eyes are wide open. Then we try to camouflage or hide our sin by ignoring it or brushing it under the rug. We find ourselves in our churches, singing songs and listening to sermons, but underneath the surface, sin is breeding in our lives.

Instead of covering our sin with our own devices, let's go to Him broken by them, allowing each one to be exposed by His light. Sin hidden is like mold ignored. As long as it stays in the dark, it incubates and multiplies. But did you know that UV light has been used to kill mold? Light, His light, will destroy the control sin has over us! May we repent and turn away completely from sin that wishes to destroy us. I believe Adam would encourage us to do the same.

Father, the Word You are releasing today is a stern call to return to You and holy living. I thank You that anything You command, You make it possible to do. You told us to "be holy for I am holy." I thank You that "holy" means "set apart." You are calling us to a new consecration and submission to You, and we embrace it. In Jesus' name, we pray. Amen!

Friday Back to the Beginning: Adam and Eve

When discovering a new topic, it helps me to study the opposite of that subject. For example, if I were learning about heat, it would be good to understand the cold. If I were learning about acids, I would need to learn about bases. Many people learn how to do something by seeing people do it the wrong way. Today I feel pressed to provide a contrast from the world opposite our ideal.

As we've learned, our goal is to recognize and execute our dual position of sitting with Christ and ruling over the enemy. But many of us find our daily lives far from this reality. I would like to expose the enemy's plan over you today! It is when he is exposed that he is immediately weakened and can be taken out much easier. He is a liar and a hider.

Remember, he executed two tricks in the garden. He lied to Eve and said, "Ye shall not surely die," in Genesis 3:4 and hid in the form of a serpent. His tricks are the same today. The Lord has great intentions for your life. He has a plan and a purpose, but so does Satan! And we need to be fully aware of it. The Lord's vision for you includes resting with Christ in heavenly places, ruling over the enemy on the earth, and walking in the love and power of the Holy Spirit! The enemy's plan for you is to be *seated* and to *rule* as well; however, the outcome of his plan is vastly different. Allow me to explain.

The enemy wants you sitting down, not in Heaven but here on the earth. He wants you low to the ground in your perspective so that every circumstance will tower over you. He doesn't want you seated in *rest*, but he wants you sitting in *complacency*. No two words are further apart! But the enemy has a way of blurring lines and making things gray. Remember, he tricks those whose eyes are off the Lord. Secondly, he wants us ruling, yes, but over what? God has called us to rule over the earth, over sin, and over the enemy. Satan would have us ignore that mandate and, instead, choose to rule over ourselves. But we were never called to do that. God alone is to rule over us. A king only has authority to rule over his jurisdiction; likewise, we've not been given authorization over ourselves to rule. Satan always twists God's plan for us! He desires for us, like Eve, to make our own decisions apart from God. He wants us to allow the lust of the flesh—*that fruit looks yummy*—the lust of the eyes—*that fruit looks beautiful*—and the pride of life—*that fruit will make me wise*—to rule every decision. His strategy is for us to live independent of God and always reach for the forbidden fruit.

Anything God has, Satan has a counterfeit! God created the world with His words, while Satan created a "big bang" with his lies. God has prophets that share His words to the people, while Satan has false prophets that shut down the true move of God. God gave the Holy Spirit to empower us, while Satan uses his foul spirits to enslave us. You see where I'm going with this?

We cannot settle for Satan's counterfeit *anything* in our lives. We want God's plan for us, nothing less. Although Satan is urging us to sit down, take a load off, and give up, God is calling us up to sit with Christ. One chair is full of apathy, while the other is full of anointing. One was fashioned with the comfort of our flesh in mind, while the other was shaped with the affliction His flesh endured for us! Do you see the huge difference? The enemy is poking at us non-stop to take over rule and reign of our lives. However, we were never called to rule over ourselves! We were called to submit to God and to rule over Satan. He is very skilled at manipulation and distortion of the truth. May we ask the Lord for wisdom and freely receive by faith the ability to see through the facade. And once exposed, may we cut off the head of the enemy in our lives by casting down every single lie that he has sent. Today is a day of freedom! Receive it! Rise from the seat of indifference and pick up your sword!

Jesus, I giggle with joy when I think about how much smarter than the enemy You are! We ask for wisdom, according to James 1:5, and know that You freely give! Remind us of the strategies of the enemy, how he uses lies as his entry points…every time! Remind us of the strategy that You possess! Eve was defeated in a garden, but You were victorious in Your garden. You did not sit down and take it easy. You kept Heaven on your mind and the Father in Your eyes. You did not rule over Your own self as You desired to have the cup of suffering removed. But instead, You uttered the most beautiful words, "Not my will, but thine be done." Then in going to the Cross, You demonstrated a life laid down before the Father. And finally, in the Resurrection, You took the scepter of rule over the earth back and stripped the enemy bare. Because You sat down in Heaven, we can too. And because You ruled over the enemy, we can. We love you, Lord, and celebrate Your power today. In Jesus' name, we pray. Amen.

Saturday Scot's Story

(photo and story approved for use by S. Mann)

*He heals the brokenhearted and binds up
their wounds* (Psalm 147:3, NIV)

Once Paul and I attended a service out of town. During the worship time, a lady received healing of a large mass on her neck. She was crying hysterically and had a look of amazement on her face. A few days later, I was hanging around after service at our local church when a gentleman approached me. He began to tell me about how his girlfriend broke up with him and how he had this tumor on his spinal cord. Immediately, the Lord revealed to me that he was convinced that this tumor would kill him. So I told him, "Scot, you think this is going to kill you?" He looked at me, eyes wide open, and shook his head as he said, "Yes." He began telling me how he's been completing his bucket list because he knows he will soon die. I then spoke the truth over him that he would "live and *not* die." Next, I turned my attention to the tumor. "Scot, we're going to pray, and you are going to be healed of this tumor." He gave me a perplexed look. I then spoke these words, "You don't think you have *enough* faith for this, do you?" He said, "No." "We're going to go on our faith, Scot, just receive!" There was a Holy Spirit boldness that came over me as I spoke these words. He sat down, and we put our hands on his neck and said, "Tumor, go in Jesus' name…right now!" We spoke to the mountain! I did not feel anything. Scot did not feel anything. But it is what happened next that still amazes me!

After leaving the church, he went to the gas station to fill his tank. As he stood in the winter air that night, a stranger approached him. This unnamed man began talking to Scot by saying, "The girl that you thought loved you did not, but the three people you just left told you the truth. Listen to what they said. God has big plans for you." As he walked away, Scot said that heat began to overtake his body. Keep in mind it was February and quiet cold out. He told me that he knew healing was flowing in that moment.

In the following days, his neck began to swell. This was the opposite of what he had expected, so he went to the doctor. The doctor opened that spot in the back of his neck, and all that was present was drainage. Scot sent me an e-mail, very excited that the mass was gone. And I told him that if it did not swell, he may never have known that it disappeared. That mass dissolved!

Today's Lesson: God heals! It's what He does. Are you willing to step out and cross the chicken line to pray over someone? Be the one who speaks to mountains, releases life, and fears nothing as you obey the Lord! Remember your job is the believing and speaking. His job is the performance!

Sunday Bella's Story

May my cry come before You, Lord; give me understanding accord-
ing to Your Word. May my supplication come before You; deliver
me according to Your promise (Psalm 119:169-170, NIV)

Bella is our third child. She always struggled with eczema, a skin
condition that causes itching, redness, and scarring. Being a person
of faith, I prayed over her skin many times. I noticed no difference
over the years; in fact, it worsened. Her arms and legs got to the point
that they were becoming scarred and would not tan like the rest of
her skin. She scratched during the day but mostly at night as she
slept. To top off this problem, Bella also endured feelings of being

left out or *rejected* within our family. She would make comments like, "Mommy, do you love me like you love the other kids?" We fought a constant battle of trying to convince her of our love. Years went on like this.

One night, while in prayer, I heard the Lord say, "Go to Bella, and I will give you the words to pray over her." It was about midnight, so I was the only one awake. I went into her bedroom, laid my hands on her, and waited. It went something like this, "Holy Spirit, I've prayed for this child for years out of my intellect, quoting all the right verses. That hasn't worked. I need you to say the very words to bring her miracle." Then as I waited, approximately sixty seconds, the Lord spoke...through me! "I command the Spirit of Rejection to get out of my daughter right now! I release God's love and acceptance to her right now." The prayer took ten whole seconds. I did not feel anything when I prayed it, and I was taken aback by the words. I thought I was here to pray over her skin. After saying this diminutive prayer, I went to bed.

What I began to notice the following days was astounding. Not only did Bella's skin begin to become new, but she also started saying things like, "Mommy, I know you love me!" She was no longer crying out for attention. She began transforming before our eyes. After about three days, her skin was totally brand-new!

Today's Lesson: Don't just pray random words because they sound right. If your prayers are not getting results, begin to wait on the Lord for keys in prayer! It's worth the wait!

Monday Joshua and Consecration

As we continue to discover our position in Christ, let's look at the life of Joshua. I love Joshua. There's so much to learn about being a leader from him. But before he ever led, he understood what it meant to be a faithful follower. He had, what I like to call, humble strength. When the spies were sent in to scope out the Promised Land, Joshua was fearless and strong. He saw with God's eyes that day! Man saw giants. God *and* Joshua saw the land! He saw victory before the battle started. Joshua was also humble in his faithfulness to Moses. When others sinned against God by turning against Moses, Joshua didn't. When others rebelled against Moses's leadership, Joshua didn't. After Moses died, the candidate for new leader was obvious! Joshua had submitted to God, stayed strong in the faith, and supported Moses entirely for forty years. It was now promotion time!

We've all heard about the story of Jericho from Joshua 6. Our kids can quote it from Sunday school, how those walls came down with a shout! But few of us know about the story in Joshua 5. Joshua had a call on his life, the same call that's on our lives. He was called to closeness with God and authority over his enemies. For this reason, his life can teach us to walk in the same calling. It was almost time for their first battle. They had crossed over the Jordan and were entering a land promised to their people all the way back to Abraham. Among some, I'm sure, excitement stirred. While others may have been fighting fear, Joshua stood resolute. He knew what God had promised, He would provide. But before the people could take on

Jericho, or even receive specific strategy from the Lord, something had to be done.

> At that time the Lord said to Joshua, *"Make flint knives for yourselves, and circumcise the sons of Israel"* (Joshua 5:2).

And Joshua obeyed.

Why is this important for us today? We have all been told of a Promised Land flowing with milk and honey. This is the place of abundance of His presence in our lives. Let's put on those awesome spiritual glasses we have for a minute! We've been told of a place of being seated with Christ and ruling over the enemy. This is our heritage. But many of us haven't taken the step of consecration to get there. Joshua could not move forward until the people were circumcised, a picture of consecration or cutting away of *self.* We too have received a call to consecration. We are to be holy, set apart, and sanctified. May we encounter Jesus and allow him to circumcise our hearts in preparation to defeat our enemy! On a side note, the Hebrew word for Jesus and Joshua is identical and means *Savior.* There's no one who knows about consecration more than our Jesus, and He is fully able to bring that reality into our hearts as well!

May we hear the rattle of the walls of our Jericho as we determine to be set apart for Christ!

Father, open our eyes to see the ways that we look like the world. We are to be in the world but not of the world. Help us realize that our destiny will be stunted if we hold onto things we've been called to let go of. I pray that Joshua 5 stays in the forefront of our thinking today as sin tries to take hold of us. May we trust and obey everything You say so that we can see that Promised Land! In Jesus' name, we pray. Amen.

Tuesday Joshua and Courage

Joshua understood the importance of consecration. In Joshua 5, he took on the difficult task of circumcising the males of the nation of Israel before taking the land of Jericho. Before Israel went into the land of promise, this cleansing ritual was completed. In order for us to enter into our Promised Land, we must endure the same cutting away. However, our circumcision is of the heart. We are to be separated or severed from our sinful desires by the knife of the Word of God! In many circles, *consecration* is a word that has been frowned upon. This is quite sad to me, for I know the power of a set-apart one! I would desire that we all get back to the importance of being Christlike. The goal of this entire study, in a nutshell, is to know who we are in God and act accordingly. There are people who have done this well, such as Joshua, and others that failed miserably, such as Adam and Eve. We can learn from them all! Today let's look at another great characteristic of Joshua. Joshua was not only consecrated; he was also courageous!

"Only be thou strong and very courageous" (Joshua 1:7a)

Moses had died, and the charge was given to Joshua to cross the Jordan and seize the land! In Joshua 1:3, the Lord declares that everywhere Joshua's feet tread is his! Isn't this just lovely? Doesn't it remind you of Genesis when God gave Adam dominion? This is an awesome depiction of Joshua's *ruling on the Earth*! Then the Lord gave Joshua authority over his enemies, "Not any man be able to stand before thee," in verse 5. Joshua's enemies were people, ours are principalities and powers, aka Satan's ranking forces (see Ephesians 6:12). Studying the warfare strategies given to Joshua to defeat his enemies, we can learn to better fight our spiritual foe! Consecration and courage were integral parts of the impending victory for Joshua!

The task before Joshua was a monumental one. Many would have collapsed under the pressure and ran, but not Joshua! The Lord was fully aware of the enormity of the call. He was not unaware of the magnitude of what He was commanding Joshua to do. But of course, He knew of His magnanimous ability to help Joshua! (Yes, it's a real word!) So the Lord, in His sweet ability to relate to fragile mankind, gave this awesome instruction: Be strong and courageous! Not once, not twice, but three times God repeats Himself to Joshua in one conversation.

"Only be thou strong and very courageous." (Joshua 1:7a)

"Have not I commanded thee? Be strong and of a good courage." (Joshua 1:9a)

"Only be strong and courageous!" (Joshua 1:18b)

This is quite significant, as the number three is symbolic of completion. God left no room for misinterpretation. He spoke a word that challenged Joshua to shun his physical senses and walk with his spiritual eyes, just like us! He knew Joshua  was up for the task. The Lord did not forget Joshua's courage forty years prior when scoping out the Promised Land. Joshua was ready to charge in while the others, except for Caleb, retreated in fear. But now, Moses was no longer at the helm. Joshua was in the proverbial driver's seat. The Lord knew the frailty of his human heart. He knows our hearts as well. Maybe we found ourselves forty years ago ready to take on Hell with a water pistol and the blood of Jesus. But today, worn by life and the death of our *Moses*, fear has crept in. I pray this study will challenge us, like Joshua, to take the command of the Lord seriously. When He says, "Be strong and courageous," it is not a suggestion. God's instructions are always commands. Yes, our enemy is fierce, yes, our circumstances are towering, but our God promised to be with us. Therefore, what do we have to fear?[2]

Father, I thank You for people like Joshua that we have to learn from. When we open the Word, help us see ourselves in these stories. We reflect that these "superheroes" of the faith were real people, just like us. God, I pray we depend solely on You and Your promise to be with us. God, may courage rise right now in everyone's heart and explode out of their mouths. Remind us that courageous people speak with COURAGE. Defeat is not in our vocabulary unless we are discussing Satan's position. May we look at every mountain and see it leveled and then speak to it unafraid. Mountain, MOVE in Jesus' name! God, give us the courage of Jesus, that when He faced the cross, He did not cower in fear. Lord, I know that relationship with You brings courage. Bring us in closer as we wait upon You. In Jesus' name, we pray. Amen.

Wednesday Joshua and Leadership

Now then we are ambassadors for Christ... (2 Corinthians 5:20a).

Although we are permeated with weaknesses and faults, we are still called to represent the Lord. Wow, what a mighty and humbling call we've been issued! Joshua understood this firsthand. He was at Moses' side forty years watching up close. He learned how to succeed as a leader and also how to get it wrong as leader. Joshua took his life lessons seriously. We see him soaring as the second leader of the newly freed nation of Israel.

Yesterday, the focus of discussion was Joshua's courage. The Lord spoke the same words over the new leader three times during one conversation: *"Be strong and courageous"* (Joshua 1:7, 9, and 18). Fast-forward to Joshua 10:25. This is where it gets good! y'all!

> *And Joshua **said** unto them, "Fear not, nor be dismayed, be **strong** and of good **courage:** for thus saith the Lord do to all your enemies against whom ye fight."*

My paraphrase goes like this:

"Gents, don't worry about a thing. Rise up, boys! God is with us. Pity your enemies because they are about to meet your God!"

Isn't this awesome? In Joshua 1, we find God encouraging Joshua. But in Joshua 10, we find *God* encouraging the people! "Hold on, April," you may say, "you said that wrong. It was *Joshua* encouraging the people." I would present to you that it was *God* encouraging the people *through* Joshua! That Word of the Lord spoken three times over Joshua had gotten down in his heart and taken root. Remember, the Word of the Lord is like seed planted in our hearts to yield… well…the LORD in our lives. Like in Mary's life, Jesus still wants to be birthed in mankind!

This is the true depiction of an ambassador of Christ. The goal is not to *act* like Christ by doing all the right things and saying all the right sayings. No, the goal is to *become* like Christ by spending time hearing His word over us! If Joshua had not waited to hear, "Be strong and courageous," three times and just rushed into battle, the outcome would have been a mess. We need to take a lesson from Joshua and wait to hear the Word of the Lord. Only then can we truly be an ambassador for Heaven and a leader for the church.

Allow me to insert a word of caution. Remember Moses, when instructed by God to speak to the rock, angrily struck the rock out of frustration and anger. This was a big problem for which the consequence was far-reaching. Because the people identified Moses with the Lord, Moses had to be physically separated from the position of leader to show the people God does not lose control. The reason I mention this is that we are all called to be ambassadors for Heaven, and we need reminders of the weightiness that carries. We may not reap such a severe punishment as Moses on the earth, but we will give an account for any we lead astray. The world does not read the Bible; they read us! We must represent Christ well. This is not a call to perfection, as none of us can attain that. This, rather, is a call to honesty, integrity, and humility. *When* we make mistakes or sin, we must make it evident that God was not a part of it. And when we are successful or excel, we should make it clear that we were not a part of it! Anything of worth in our lives flows from our Father.

It is imperative that we develop deep roots by meditating on the Word and soaking in His presence. Only then can we be true ambassadors of Christ. Only then can fruit be developed in our lives and become available for others to "taste and see that the Lord is good" (Psalm 34:8). Although the Bible is complete and bound in leather, there is more to the story being written. We are called by Paul *living epistles* for the world to read. You are a living book being written before men's eyes. Are they reading Christ?

Father, we hear Your call to be an ambassador. You have set us as representatives of Heaven here on the earth. May we be so rooted in You that it's Your fruit on our branches. May we get our eyes off the vessel of who we are and focus on what fills the vessel…You! Lord, fill us with love for Your Word, Your presence, and Your power. You are our leader! Jesus, You proved to be the perfect ambassador of Heaven by walking in perfect humility and love. Help us, Holy Spirit, to follow in the footsteps of our leader who, unlike Moses, never represented the Father poorly. May the blood of Jesus cover our mistakes, the grace of Jesus empower us forward, and the love of Jesus fuel our every move. Lord, we pray all this in Jesus' name. Amen.

Thursday Joshua and Warfare

*For Joshua drew not his hand back, wherewith he stretched out
the spear, until he had utterly destroyed all* (Joshua 8:26a).

The enemy is real!

And he is a real threat if we do not act accordingly. Today we will
focus on Joshua's ability to engage in warfare against his enemy. God
made a promise to Israel that He would place them in a land, a land
of their own. The time had come, and Joshua was the man to take
them there. They spent four hundred years in Egyptian bondage,
were rescued at the hand of Moses, and had lived in the desert for
the previous forty years. Faith-filled and ready to move, the remaining Israelites were more than prepared. There was just one predica-
ment. The land was inhabited. Joshua's enemy was sleeping in his
bed, living in his home, and farming his land. This is significant
for us because our enemy (spiritual glasses on!) is doing the same in
our lives. This reminds us that although God gives the promise and
shows us the way to it, we have a role to play! We are called to kick
the enemy out!

Joshua had encountered his enemy once before…forty years
before. He wasn't swayed then, and he wouldn't be swayed now. Fear
could not grip Joshua as God had already provided a word three
times to "fear not, take courage." With the Word of God in hand,
Joshua was ready to go. There was a God-given tenacity, a warrior
spirit in Joshua. We know this power today as the Holy Spirit.

> *For God has not given us a spirit of fear; but of power,*
> *love, and a sound mind* (2 Timothy 1:7)

We have been fully equipped to face our giants and utterly destroy them all, just like Joshua. This mighty man of valor was successful time and time again against the enemy and cleared out the land for Israel. Why? His connection to the Lord was his lifeline of strength. Frequently, he would take counsel from the Lord, knowing that on his own he was not strong enough. He would become charged in the Lord's presence.

Joshua did not show his enemy mercy. As Joshua 8:26 says, he *utterly destroyed all.* This is our mandate as well. Our enemy is sly and has invaded our territory. Although through Christ we've been given back our authority to rule on the earth, the enemy doesn't give it up easily. Remember, the promises of God are conditional. Everything from the Lord is only received by faith, and faith without works or action is dead.

I see the body of Christ with a deed in hand sealed with the mark of Heaven. In it is promised health, salvation, freedom, joy, peace, life, love, deliverance, and victory. It is signed with the blood of Jesus. And the church holds this deed in her hand, waving it around Sunday after Sunday, saying, "Look what I have!" We sing about it, preach about it, learn about it, and then we go home, and our lives are anything but what we rejoiced in on Sunday. We hold the deed, but the Devil holds the keys! And this angers me!

> *Thou therefore, my son, be strong in the grace that is in*
> *Christ Jesus...No man that wars entangles himself with*
> *the affairs of this life; that he may please him who hath*
> *chosen him to be a soldier* (2 Timothy 2:1, 4)

When we become entangled with things of this world such as strife, jealousy, bitterness, hate, anxiety, frustration, worry, condemnation, etc., we cannot take the keys from the enemy. Our position is to rule on the earth. Owning the keys is a picture of ruling over a home. The Lord has defeated the enemy and taken the keys from him that Adam lost. And what did Jesus do with those keys? He handed them right back to us!

> *"I will give you the keys of the kingdom of*
> *heaven..."* (Matthew 16:19a)

Let's rise up like Joshua and walk with a holy disdain for the enemy. We must stop being entertained on his playground, of the world, and cast him out of our lives. Remember, you already have the document from Heaven signed by the judge.

> *Freedom* is yours today!

That is your Promised Land, a place of total freedom to worship your God, void of Satan's chains upon your back. Be like Joshua! Be like Jesus! They walked in freedom and brought others to that same realization. Do the same today!

Father, I thank You now for this Word. I know that You are never taken unaware by the enemy's tactics. I ask You to make me like Joshua, always arrayed in full battle gear. Remind me each morning to dress myself spiritually, in the armor You have provided. Right now, aloud I say, "I put on the helmet of salvation, the belt of truth, the breastplate of righteousness, and the sandals of peace. I hold the shield of faith to quench every fiery dart of the enemy and hold the Sword of the Spirit to cut his head off." You have provided everything I need to walk in victory. May I come under Your shadow once more and remain in that place of safety and power. I love you, Lord! In Jesus' name, in His authority, I pray. Amen.

Friday Joshua and Praise

As I was seeking the Lord this morning, He spoke to me by saying, "The word of the day is *praise*." I love having a God that is personal and speaks to those with ears to hear! I've been meditating on *praise* today. As I began to ponder what the theme of today's devotion would be, it became very clear, *Joshua* and *praise*. Throughout this week, we've looked at Joshua's consecration, courage, leadership, and his warfare. Today let's examine the importance of praise in Joshua's life.

> *And Joshua called the priests, and said unto them, "Take up the ark of the covenant, and let seven priests bear seven trumpets of ram's horns before the ark of the Lord"* (Joshua 6:6)

We all know the story of Jericho. It's a wonderful story. We talk about it in Sunday school, sing about the walls coming down, and might even do a Jericho March around church. At least, that's what we did when I was growing up! But I wonder if many of us have ever thought about Jericho in more depth. God instructed an inexperienced leader, facing a fortified enemy, to fight essentially by walking and shouting. And let's not forget that before all this would occur, Joshua played surgeon and circumcised all the males. That, my friends, was a strategy for war that did not originate in a human mind. Many a soul would have responded to God with, "Um…God…are You serious? Do You really want me to take a multitude of people and just walk around walls for six days and on the seventh, shout and blow trumpets…really?" We all know the story, and therefore, we know the outcome. But Joshua hadn't read Joshua 6 yet! However, he acted swiftly to obey God. This immediate obedience was an amazing indicator of his faith. We can learn so much from Joshua!

Joshua proved his understanding of the power of praise by engaging in God's plan fully. I believe a life given in obedience is full of praise! Every time we bow to God's will and not our own, our life is magnifying the Lord. Remember, although unseen, there is a spiritual realm that is affected by our actions. When our life silently obeys God, there is a shout released in the unseen world! When we lay down *self* and submit to a plan that makes no sense, "Hallelujahs" are ringing from our heart upward. And Joshua did just that! He trusted the plan that removed his logic and reasoning. He obeyed, believing that shouts and horn blasts would level a wall, and he was right!

Obedience is praise!

Anything that exalts Jesus is praise! Oh, that we would comprehend the mysteries of God deeper than surface level. Praise is *more* than singing and clapping. That is a form of praise, and an awesome one at that! But praise flows from a heart before it flows from a mouth.

The Biblical Law of First Mention tells us that a doctrine's first occurrence, Biblically speaking, gives much insight into the meaning of that principle.[4]

Do you know the first time the word *praise* is mentioned? In Genesis 29:35, Leah, Jacob's first wife, bore her fourth son. *"And she conceived again, and bare a son; and she said, 'Now will I praise the Lord;' therefore she called his name Judah; and left bearing."* I love this for so many reasons! First, I love it because *I* have a fourth-born son named Judah. Secondly, I love this because there's more to this verse than meets the eye. In verses 32-34, Leah has three sons—Reuben, Simeon, and Levi. Names in that time were more significant in meaning than today. I believe we can gain so much insight from the meaning of the names of Leah's four sons. You see, long story short, her husband was tricked into marrying her. He really wanted her

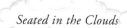
sister, Rachel, whom he ended up getting some years later. Needless to say, Leah's self-esteem was less than great. Let's learn from this wife of Jacob.

Genesis 29
#1 Reuben: Verse 32 *"Now my husband will love me."*
#2 Simeon: Verse 33 *"The Lord has heard that I was hated."*
#3 Levi: Verse 34 *"Now this time will my husband be joined unto me."*
#4 Judah: Verse 35 *"NOW I PRAISE THE LORD"*
...and she left bearing.

Wow! Did you catch that? The first three were all named out of *her* pain, *her* rejection, *her* lack. But Judah was named with complete focus on the Lord. Nothing about Leah or her circumstances dictated Judah's naming. She finally came to the place after her third son that no matter what she faced, the Lord was worthy to be praised! When we begin to praise Him regardless of what is going on in our lives, we can do like Leah and *leave bearing.* She had been attempting to please and win over her husband by bearing these children. Simply put, this is a temptation for us all (spiritual glasses on, please). If we abandon praise focusing solely on ourselves and our situations, we will enter a never-ending season of "bearing." This is action trying to receive something from man that only God can give. The Lord had already approved Leah! The Bible says He *blessed* her by opening her womb. Every time she toiled for Jacob's affection, the Lord was standing there with His arms outstretched. When she cried over the lackluster love of Jacob, the Lord was there with love welling in His eyes for her.

Bearing says, "If I do enough, if I'm good enough, someone will accept me."

NO MORE!

We need to abandon this thinking. Let's go ahead and birth our *Judah* of praise now! When we live with that kind of praise flowing, like Joshua, we will see walls crumble, rivers split, and the sun stand still. We will see victory as we lift His name!

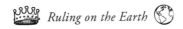

Jesus came from the lineage of Judah…not by chance. He's also called a Lion. He *roars* upon our praise!

Father, You know our frail state. You see the moments of desperation as we long to be loved and accepted by others. Rejection and abandonment wait at our bedside each morning to begin their torment. We are much like Leah and try, try, and try again to bear what we think we must to get what we think we need from others. God, I thank You today for the fresh perspective on praise that You've given. Praising You is the way to victory! It's the way to dig out of every pit. Praise is a weapon that we can no longer afford to leave in our bunker. God, I ask that You would ignite a fire in each of us to live praise out loud. God, it's more than a song…It's a celebration of who You are! May we live with this in mind, in heart, and on our lips! In Jesus' name we, ask these things. Amen.

Saturday Provision from Above

"And new things I declare; before they spring into being I announce them to you" (Isaiah 42:9b)

The story you are about to read may be hard to conceive, but aren't all God stories that way? To preface it, I want to share that the Lord speaks to me in many different ways. He has for years. This began when I told Him I would not limit how He could speak to me. I decided to be like a little child and walk with open ears to the Lord's voice. Now we can return to the story! I was actually praying for supernatural provision to help me publish this book when I began seeing the lonely letter M. When I say I *saw* the letter M, I mean that repeatedly, more often than normal, I encountered that letter and had a perception that it was important. So I did what I always do when I perceive the Lord is speaking—I prayed. "Lord what is the significance of this letter in my life?" I felt like He said, "It's not a letter, it's a number." I was perplexed by this, so of course, I opened

Google for assistance. I quickly discovered that M is the Roman numeral for 1,000.

At this point, I still did not know what it meant, but I was on the road to discovery. I messaged a faith-friend of mine, and you can read that text above. I had been seeing the M's on mailboxes a lot. After prayer, my friend and I felt led to believe God for one thousand (M-Roman numeral) dollars (M-money) to come to my mailbox (M-mail box). We prayed this on August 18, 2016. Now I need to say this! I am not one that prays about, or even thinks about, money a whole bunch. This was the first time God has ever led me to believe for a specific amount…but He did lead!

Three days later, as I went to check the mail, I actually said… out loud, "I believe for great things in this mailbox today." At a later date, I was telling a friend this testimony, and she said, "You talk to your mailbox?" I said, "Girl, I talk to everything! After all, everything was created with words!" But I digress, so let's return to our story once more. I opened my mailbox, and there was an envelope from a lady I had never met. She had come to know about People Ablaze Ministry through our Facebook videos and web site blog. She lives ten hours away. Well, wouldn't you know it, a one-thousand-dollar check was made payable to People Ablaze Ministry. I can't say I was shocked, but boy was I excited! And here is the kicker…she wrote the check on August 18, 2016, the same day I agreed in prayer with my friend for the same amount to come into my mailbox. You can see in the photo above the text I sent along with the check date and amount. You can't make these things up!

Lesson of the Day: Think it not strange when you feel led to pray very specifically. As the above verse states, God announces things to us often before they spring up. Perhaps the reason we haven't seen the crop yield yet is because it is waiting on us to agree with God!

Sunday Story of the Butterfly

The seventy-two returned with joy, saying, "Lord, even the demons are subject to us in Your name!" (Luke 10:17, ESV)

Paul and I were at a prayer meeting one night with some friends. A young woman (I will keep her name confidential) came in and needed prayer desperately. She was physically shaking from anxiety. I could feel the fear that gripped her; it was tangible in the room. She came seeking prayer…seeking freedom. We gathered around her and began to pray. As we did, she became visually uncomfortable. We prayed over this girl for maybe an hour or so. I'm not sure, but it felt like an eternity with not visible signs of success. As a matter of fact, the more we prayed, the worse it seemed. I remember sitting back on the couch for a moment and literally lying back on Jesus. Just before I gave up praying and walked out, I heard the Holy Spirit say, "Begin to declare Jesus is Lord. Declare it over this room. Declare it over her."

I began to have utter joy flood from my being as I said repeatedly, "Jesus is Lord!" As I did this, boldness arose in me. It was no longer *April* praying; the Holy Spirit had taken over! I darted over to where she lay on the floor and, as the Lord led, cast the spirit out of her. Again, I had no idea what I was doing and had zero training, but the Holy Spirit knows all about these things! She was set free and visibly looked lighter. The next thing that happened still amazes me.

A few weeks prior to this happening, I was sketching, and the picture above is what I drew. I remember it was so ugly that I hid it with my hand as I sketched it, not knowing why I was drawing this crazy picture. On a side note, the enemy will tell you that you're crazy when you obey God. After the young woman was freed, the Lord reminded me of the tiny sketch in my journal, which I happened to have with me. I ran over to it and ripped out the drawing. I said to her, "I think I'm supposed to give you this picture." As she held the picture, the words that she said still give me chills, "This is the exact demon that is in my nightmares wrapping chains around me." The room got silent. The Lord knew two weeks prior that this young woman would be set free from this foul spirit. Later I came to know that this young lady had a suicide plan, and the prayer meeting was her final *try* at life. To this day, this young woman has blossomed into a beautiful butterfly. She teaches others about who they are in Christ and models a life surrendered to God. It has been amazing to see! She was excited about her story being shared with all of you and hope that it would encourage you that freedom is for all.

Lesson of the Day: The enemy likes to hide and be ignored, but enough is enough! It's time to kick him out of our lives once and for all. We have the authority to do so in Jesus' name!

Monday Ruling in a Foreign Land: Lessons from Joseph

Pondering moving forward in this study, the Lord brought Joseph to the forefront of my mind. I began to think about his life and the journey he took from start to finish. I became intrigued with his ability through God to rule over situations that seemed impossible. I believe we can learn so much from Joseph on how to do the same in our day. Joseph faced odds we could not begin to imagine and, in the end, prevailed over them all. He displayed qualities, in dark seasons, which gained him entrance into brighter ones. In our continued theme of being "seated in the clouds and ruling on the earth," there is much more to learn about staying in our God-given position no matter our circumstances. Joseph can help fill in more of the puzzle for us as we look deeper into his walk. Go with me now back to Genesis as we study the life of this man together.

And Pharaoh said unto his servants, "Can we find such a one as this is, a man in whom the Spirit of God is?" And Pharaoh said unto Joseph... "Thou shalt be over my house, and according unto thy word shall all my people be **ruled***: only in the throne will I be greater than thou... See, I have set thee over all the land of Egypt"* (Genesis 41:38-41)

Wow! Isn't that amazing? In the text above, Joseph is given authority to rule over all of Egypt directly under the Pharaoh. Never before had a man of God found himself in this type of position in a *worldly* kingdom. However, Joseph's journey to the palace was anything but royal. Let's journey years back before the palace. In Genesis

37, we note Joseph's father showing him favor by giving him a coat of many colors. This did not sit well with Joseph's ten brothers.

*And when his brethren saw that their father loved him
more than all his brethren, they hated him, and could
not speak peaceably (unto him)* (Genesis 37: 4)

Unfortunately, it went from bad to worse for Joseph when, in the very next verse, Joseph shared a dream. He told his brothers of their grain stalks bowing before his. Those boys were getting quite heated at this point. "So you're telling us you think your puny self is going to rule over us? Are you kidding me? You're the youngest and the least," (April's paraphrase version). So Joseph does what any sane person would do—pun intended—he tells them of another dream where the sun, moon, and eleven stars bow before him. By the way, Joseph would later have an eleventh brother added! This second dream was the last straw for these jealous brothers.

Joseph had been given amazing favor with his father, both heavenly and earthly, and it angered people. God's favor continues to illicit this response today. Joseph was about to encounter a world far separated from the one he had known. The life of Joseph is very rich, and there's much to be learned from it. Much of his journey parallels the life of Jesus.

*And when they saw him afar off, even before he came near unto
them, they conspired against him to slay him. And they said one
to another, "Behold, this dreamer cometh"* (Genesis 37:18-19)

Thank the Lord for Reuben, the eldest son. He stopped the plot to murder the boy, and the decision was made to throw him in a pit instead. When Reuben returned to the pit and found it empty, he ripped his clothes and mourned. When his back was turned, Joseph was sold into slavery for twenty pieces of silver by the others. Jesus was sold by His Jewish *brother*, Judas, for thirty!

There seems to be a theme in the lives of God's called-out ones. A point of rejection, usually by ones quite close, is encountered. We are dreamers! Many are not. We skip through life wearing our coat of many colors from the Lord. Many are tied up in a life of toil in the fields. We receive God's love freely apart from our actions. Many are trying to earn the Father's love by works, which is rooted in fear ... fear of not being enough, doing enough, or having enough. I have been reminded again and again: do not fear. But the Lord has taken it further by speaking, "Do not fear *man*." Recently, He led me to this beautiful verse that I hadn't *seen* before.

> *Stop regarding man in whose nostrils is breath,*
> *for of what account is he?* (Isaiah 2:22)

Doesn't that say it all? Fear of man is a mountain that will stand in our way of pleasing God...every time. Although man has the power to ridicule our dreams, hate us because of God's favor, and throw us in a pit, they do not have power over our soul! When we are accustomed to praise from others, love being poured out toward us, and acceptance, we need to ready ourselves. The foreign ground of jealousy is just ahead. The unfamiliar pit of persecution may be being dug at this very minute.

I am not attempting to discourage or depress us. My goal is to speak the Word of the Lord as I hear it. This is a warning to get rid of *man-pleasing* from our hearts. God wants us totally reliant on Him and what He thinks concerning us alone. Too many of us, including myself, have had ***approval addiction*** and fear of man far too long. Today is the day we decide to cut off the head of the enemy. If he can keep us subservient to the opinion of others, then when the time comes to take that leap of faith, we will miss it. Joseph landed in a pit because of his purpose in God to rule. But as we will learn, Joseph's God was faithful to him, and he didn't stay in that pit. Many times the pit becomes an opportunity. It's in that hard place that we make the decision to *live* for God's pleasure alone! Even if your dream gets you thrown into a pit, no worries! It will ultimately lead you to the palace!

Father, it's not Your will for us to walk in fear of man anymore! Lord, Proverbs 29:25 tells us that "the fear of man brings a snare, but who-

ever trusts in the Lord shall be safe." And we do not want to fall in that trap anymore. We want to trust in You! It seems that the two—fear of man and trust in You—are opposing forces in our lives. Today we choose the right path. We make a decision to obey You in every area without being paralyzed by fear of man any longer. God, I also call out the lie of **approval addiction** *in every reader. I rebuke, bind, and cast out that foul stronghold! We will never come to a place in You, soaring like the eagle, when we are tied down to man's opinion. Set us free today, Holy Spirit! We praise and thank You for freedom! In Jesus' name, we pray. Amen.*

Tuesday Ruling in a Foreign Land: Lessons from Joseph

Today we continue to look at the life of Joseph. So far, we've contrasted Adam and Joshua. One forfeited authority on the earth to Satan and the other took the bull by the horns and led God's people into their promised land. In looking at Joseph, we see a different type of man from Joshua. His life doesn't read as much of a war cry like Joshua's, but there are other lessons we can learn from him.

Joseph stayed calm in desperate situations. He walked in obedience no matter the cost. Finding himself in a foreign country, he maintained his character. He was thrown in a pit and a prison, he was lied about and mocked; however, *who he was* did not change. As a matter of fact, in these *tight* places, his character was magnified. Our lives are no different! We wake up each day and find ourselves in *Egypt*. Although we are *of* the Kingdom of God, we live *in* Egypt. Our land has become dark and corrupt, and sometimes we feel like a prisoner in our own *free* country. But today I am encouraging us to remember, no matter where we live, we are seated with Christ in heavenly places!

Let's dive more into Joseph's story, shall we?

*And Joseph was brought down to Egypt; and Potiphar, an **offi-cer** of Pharaoh, captain of the guard, an Egyptian, bought him of the hands of the Ishmaelites...* (Genesis 39:1a)

Did you know the word *officer* used in the above verse comes from the Hebrew word *cariyc?* Now you may be asking, "What does that have to do with anything?" I asked the Lord the same thing when He had me look up the origin; that was until I discovered the meaning in the original language. Here's my relentless plug to begin using a *Strong's Concordance*. The word *cariyc* means a eunuch or to castrate.[5]

Scholars are mixed on their opinions on whether or not Potiphar was an actual eunuch or not, but we are going to look deeper than the physical (spiritual glasses on, please!) Here comes Joseph, a strapping, fertile young man. He was endowed with favor from God, as we read below.

> *And the Lord was with Joseph, and he was a prosperous man, and he was in the house of his master the Egyptian. And his master saw that the Lord was with him, and that the Lord made* **all** *that he did to prosper in his hand* (Genesis 39:2-4)

Potiphar placed Joseph over his entire house, and his house was blessed because of Joseph. But then verse 7 falls like a sledgehammer.

> *Joseph's master's wife cast her eyes upon Joseph, and she said, "Lie with me."*

I can just hear the gulp in Joseph's throat. He is in a good place with his master. I'm sure he had been anticipating his destiny, remembering those dreams of grandeur. Now this woman standing before him was going to ruin it all. He knew he had two options:

1.) Consent to the enemy's plan, remaining comfortable and safe

or

2.) Deny the advances of the enemy and be subject to the pit again

Joseph was quick to respond in obedience. His character was not shaken by this temptation. Let's face it. He was a man and was probably legitimately tempted physically to comply. I think too often we strip away the humanness of these Biblical characters, but he *was* a man.

What did she see in Joseph? Whether her husband was a physical eunuch or not is of no consequence to the case in point. In her eyes, as evidenced by her lust for Joseph, Potiphar was impotent. This can relate to us spiritually because there is a world full of men and women that have titles but no real power to back it up. They are spiritual eunuchs. The enemy can spot them a mile away. They carry preeminence and significance before man's eyes but are totally barren, spiritually speaking. Satan often leaves these alone, as they are of no threat to him. He wants them comfortable with title alone. Pomp and circumstance are their native languages. However, his goal is to target the ones like Joseph, who carry real potency in the spirit, and strip them...us...of this by temptation. The story of Potiphar's wife reminds me of Adam's temptation all over again. The enemy puts things pleasing to the eyes in front of us and says, "Look, look at it. Keep looking at it. Now take and eat."

Lord, help us be like Joseph and run the other way. Doesn't this seem to mirror David's life as well? David had the favor of God upon him, and it gained him favor with King Saul...temporarily. This seems to be a trend in our pilgrimage as well. Remember the same Saul that loved David later tried to kill him...multiple times. Remember the same crowd that cried, "Hosanna," later shouted, "Crucify." Moments like these will come for us all. If we are bound by man-pleasing, we will be tossed around like tumbleweed. It's a trap every time. Just like a mouse lured to its death with yummy cheese and then—*smack!*—so is the person who thrives on the praises of man. In the end, it's always *smack!*

The Lord wants us readied. There's a world out there full of Egyptians. Their living is foreign to us. Their ways are not our ways, but many times they receive us joyfully because of the favor on our lives. They celebrate us, they shout, "Hosanna," to our king. But then comes the turning. There is a moment of crisis where they either join us in this walk of faith or turn away. Our message is not always pleasant to hear. Sometimes the Lord has us, like Joseph, to shun sin or call it out. This turns the once loving Potiphar into the very one who would throw us in prison. Why did Potiphar do such a thing? Jealousy! Admiration turned to jealousy, and it did so quickly.

We must shun evil at all costs. We will hear things like, "Who do they think they are...holier than thou? They think they have it all together." But I pray that we will remain, like Joseph, calm, humble, and full of courage to obey regardless of the cost. May we value God's opinion supremely in our lives and act accordingly!

Lord, You are our Father. You are also the Father of Joseph. You watched his journey and led him at each turn. I love the fact that everywhere he found himself, You prospered him. Teach our hearts to obey. We want to be transformed in the depths of who we are. When we are in a pit, we will magnify You. The pit is a lonely place, but You are there! I thank you that in the pit, only one thing is visible…the sky! We cannot see ground level circumstances anymore; all we can do is look up and see the clouds! God, remind us that we are seated in those clouds with Jesus no matter our position on the earth! We praise You in Jesus' name. Amen.

Wednesday Ruling in a Foreign Land: Lessons from Joseph and Daniel

I love the stories of Joseph and Daniel. They share so many commonalities. Let's look at a few! They both ended up in foreign lands, not by choice, and then were taken captive under the ruling power of that country. Joseph was sold into slavery in Egypt and, out of no fault of his own, was imprisoned. Daniel was taken as a boy and relocated to Babylon. Regardless of their circumstances, they were men of integrity. Both made decisions to obey God, knowing they would face punishment as a result. But it mattered not to them. Daniel was thrown in a pit of lions for praying, and Joseph in a prison for shunning evil. This dynamic duo's similarities do not stop there! They both landed in their pits, due to jealousy, from close relationships. They had favor with leaders and excelled at everything they did. Consequently, they were both charged with ruling over groups of people and tasks. Shall I keep going? They were both able to interpret dreams and found themselves promoted because of God's favor in this area. They learned how to endure, and even thrive, while living in heathen nations. Isn't this fascinating? On the subject of "ruling on the earth," I would be remiss to leave out these men's journeys. Let's dive in!

Through obedience, these men received keys from God. These keys helped them excel behind bars and eventually freed them from those same bars! I believe God is no respecter of persons and has the same keys for us if we'll only ask!

We left Joseph yesterday being hauled off to prison for a crime he did not commit. I find it very interesting that in Genesis 39:20

Pharaoh throws Joseph in a prison where the *king's prisoners were bound.* Although Joseph was thrown in jail, the Lord was setting him up with the right people. He would later be helped to freedom by a connection made behind those prison walls. The Lord's presence makes any jail cell a place of victory for us! Immediately after Joseph was placed in that dungeon, we see this beautiful verse:

> *But the Lord was with Joseph, and shewed him mercy, and gave him favor in the sight of the keeper of the prison. And the keeper of the prison committed to Joseph's hand all the prisoners that were in the prison* (Genesis 39:21-22a)

Although Joseph was in prison, the Lion of the Tribe of Judah was his companion!

As soon as Joseph hit that cell, he was given favor to lead. Just because he was captive in a foreign land did not mean he was not called to lead. Daniel's story reads quite parallel. His country was besieged, and the next decision of the Babylonian ruler was to hand out favor.

> *(Bring)…children in whom (is) no blemish, but well* **favored***, and skillful in all wisdom, and cunning in knowledge, and understanding science…* (Daniel 1:4a)

This act could only have been initiated by God's favor on the Hebrew boys. The favor of God overrules position, rank, age, or creed. Who would have thought that the next advisor to the Babylonian king would have been a captive Hebrew boy? No one would have predicted Joseph, the youngest and seemingly spoiled son of Jacob, to one day rule over Egypt! He wasn't even Egyptian... sounds a lot like Moses too! When God's favor rests upon an individual, nothing else matters. This favor is promised to us. We must be reminded, though, that the promises of God are always conditional. Without faith, we cannot receive them. Too many times we are anticipating praise of men when we should be seeking God's pleasure alone; only then will we find favor with the right people at the right time.

> *God...hath blessed us with all spiritual blessings in*
> *heavenly places in Christ (Ephesians 1:3b)*

Did you catch where the blessings are distributed from? They are in heavenly places with Christ. He holds our every blessing, including God's favor. Our relationship with Him is of utmost importance. Otherwise, we will hide from the "open window" and abandon our prayers. We will, unlike Joseph, take the "forbidden fruit" presented to us. Christ is our key...to everything! There's no "ruling on the earth" without being "seated in the clouds" with Jesus *first!*

Father, we are intrigued by the lives of these two men. Thank you for recording their lives, in the Bible, by the power of the Holy Spirit for us to glean from. As we've found ourselves living in current-day Egypt and Babylon, we desire to make good decisions like they did. Evil appears to be ruling the land and growing darker each day. But, God, we remember Joseph and Daniel! They lived out humility and service. Even in that evil land, they showed love. May we do as they did and serve our fellowman. Like Joseph, teach us to be selfless in our ministry one to another. He interpreted the dreams of two prisoners and did not find freedom for two additional years. May we reveal Jesus any way we can, even if our bringing freedom to others doesn't get us out of prison. Make us like Daniel with a submissive respect for those in authority, even the evil ones. Help us to pray for our leaders and, when ridiculed, stay humble. Wipe away all pride from us so that we will be graceful with the favor You pour out.

We ask for the ability to stay seated with Christ, remembering He is our goal and our prize! He is the only one we seek favor with. In Jesus' name, we pray. Amen.

Fun Similarities:

Joseph and Daniel
1. Taken to a foreign land against their will
2. Placed in bondage in a heathen nation
3. Men of integrity and consecration
4. Obeyed God knowing they would be punished for it
5. Daniel denied the king's "fancy" food, Joseph denied the kings "fancy" wife
6. Landed in pits due to jealousy
7. Dream interpretation gained listening ears with leaders
8. Given favor with foreign leaders
9. Excelled at everything they did
10. Placed in positions to rule
11. Walked in wisdom and humility

Thursday Dreams Resurrected

We are hard-pressed to find a biblical character who, before reaching their destiny in God, did not face a dark season first. I wish it were not this way, but repeatedly in Scripture we see a common theme in the lives of the *called-out* ones of God. They are given a dream, the dream is taken away, and a time of testing is endured. Once proven faithful to God regardless of the outcome, the dream is restored. We see this in so many people's lives. Let's review a few now!

ABRAHAM was promised a son but could not conceive. Later after conceiving miraculously, Abraham was tested to sacrifice his dream on the altar. He obeyed regardless of the outcome, and the dream was restored. Isaac lived, and God provided a sacrifice. Through Abraham we learn that in order for a promise to be born, it must first die. This rings true with every seed that hits the soil!

JACOB was promised a *dream* girl in Rachel, only to awake beside a different bride entirely. Laban had pulled the *ole' switcheroo*! At this point, Jacob's dream died, but Jacob held true to the prize and worked another seven years for Rachel. This was his *wilderness* season, I'm sure. Later through Leah, Rachel, and their maids, Jacob's sons were born, also known as the twelve tribes of Israel. The story of Jacob teaches us that God will use the undesirable *Leah* seasons of our life to bring about a birthing that we otherwise couldn't have conceived.

JOSEPH, as we know, had dreams of his brothers bowing down to him. He saw images of predominance and success through those dreams as a boy. Instead, he found himself in a pit, in chains, in a prison, forgotten about, and left for years. Until the day they *remembered* him. We cannot know God's thoughts concerning the two years Joseph sat in the dungeon waiting, hoping, praying. But conceivably, God could have been allowing the seed of "Joseph" to die. From Joseph we gain an understanding of the importance of patience in waiting for the dream. We learn that, however long it takes, we want to be fully readied before going to the palace.

A DAUGHTER OF LEVI, as she is called in Exodus 2, had a son. I'm sure she dreamed of caring for that baby, loving him, and teaching him the ways of the Lord. However, he was born during a period in history where the king put out an edict that all male babies must be thrown in the river and drown. I'm sure by now you have concluded that the baby was Moses. His mother's heart *sank*, but Moses would not—pun intended! She placed him in a basket and allowed the river to take him. She put him totally into the hands of God that day. Pharaoh's daughter collected him from the water and called for his own mother to nurse him. Not only did she get to take her boy home to nurse him, but she was also paid for it by the daughter of the man who wanted him dead! This unnamed woman teaches us that as the enemy is threatening to kill our dream, we should release it to God and trust Him fully.

For JOSHUA, the promise stayed buried forty years before being resurrected. RUTH went husband-less and hopeless while she waited for her kinsman redeemer in Boaz. HANNAH spent many years barren, waiting for a son of promise in Samuel. DAVID lived in a cave waiting to be king of all Israel. A WIDOW from Zarephath used her last food to make Elijah a meal before her provision came.

JOB lost it all before gaining double. The PROPHETS dreamed of a day of restoration for Israel but lived in a reality opposite that. Isaiah lost Uzziah, his king, before seeing the King of Kings. MARY's dream of her son saving His people seemed to die as she watched Him brutally killed. Of course, we all know what happened three days later…the dead seed sprouted eternal life for us all!

So what will your story be?

The dreams God has given you are just like seeds! I find no better analogy. A seed must go into a *dark place*, the ground. Our dreams are often left in obscurity, hidden from everyone but us for years. Then the seed must die. We have to get to the point that, regardless of what else God does for us or brings to us, we  will serve Him. Regardless if we lose every dream we've ever had, He is ENOUGH! He must be enough. Until we reach this place of contentment in God, the seed just lies there in the soil. It is in *this* consecration or laying down of one's will to God that the needful death occurs, and then the dream is resurrected. God's time is not our time. And although to us we've waited too long on the promise, to God it's been no time at all. Remember, Jesus' whole ministry was three years long, just three years. God can do more in less time with a consecrated vessel than a lifetime with an impure one. The prisons, pits, and deserts are all testing grounds that must be visited before destinies are birthed. Remember it was the Holy Spirit that led Jesus into the wilderness where he spent forty days (see Luke 4). But there's great news awaiting everyone that has found themselves in the pressure and obscurity of the wilderness. Look at the result that ensued after Jesus' wilderness experience was over.[8]

And Jesus returned in the power of the Spirit... (Luke 4:14a)

I'm not sure what your dream is. We all have a specific destiny and calling from the Lord, but each of our callings requires one common ingredient for success. We must all walk in the *power* of the Spirit, just like Jesus did. Let's have eyes to see beyond the *pressure* of today to the *power* of tomorrow! In order to rule and reign with Christ, we must go through this process, sometimes multiple times. Let's set our eyes like flint upon Jesus and stay positioned in Him.

Father, we ask You to strip away our "natural" sight and give us spiritual eyes. God, I ask You to pour dreams into Your people...new dreams... great dreams. Remind us that just because they appear dormant Your dreams for us never stay down. We water the soil of our lives with Your Word so that those seeds can begin to sprout up. May the sun of Your love and glory warm our hearts so we will allow ourselves to dream again. Resurrect visions! Remind us to write out the vision, make it plain, and keep it before our eyes. We thank You that You are the God of wonderful, exciting dreams. Make us full of hope, just like You Lord! In Jesus' name, we pray. Amen.

Friday Service: The Door of Destiny

The Way Up Is Down: Jesus, Joseph, and Daniel

Yesterday we pondered our dreams of old. We talked about how, for many of us, it seems as if those dreams have died. But in study, we learned that every promise must first be buried as a seed before it can be sprouted in our lives. No seed before it has died can sprout. There is not one person that hasn't received promises from God. In fact, I'd say He's promised far more than we ever claim as our own. Each believer is God's favorite, for when He looks at us, He sees His Son's sacrifice. Therefore, there is no excuse for anyone to be left hopeless. We all have a designed destiny! We all have a hope and a future in the Lord.

However, all promises of God are conditional. He does something, and we have to respond to receive from Him. For example, He died for the world, but only those who, by faith, receive His sacrifice can be saved. One key I have observed that opens the door of destiny is service. Even our Lord did not come to be served but to serve. Doesn't this speak volumes? What excuse do we have not to serve? With the cross in mind and the pain lurking in the distant future, Jesus chose to wash the feet of the disciples. I want you to think about that. When Jesus came face-to-face with humanity, the very humanity that would send Him to the cross, He humbly served them. Jesus is the express image of the Father. We can watch His life and learn how the Father would have us live ours.

Jesus served.

Journeying back to the life of Joseph, we see an amazing similarity he shares with Jesus, one of many! The very ones that captured and bought Joseph were the same ones he served. He served in Potiphar's home before being taken to a prison cell because of a false accusation. On a side note, Jesus was also taken prisoner because of false accusations from the high priest. Let's peek into the prison cell to see what Joseph occupied his time with. Two of the king's prisoners thrown in the cell with Joseph were a baker and a cup bearer.

And the captain of the guard charged Joseph with them, and he served them... (Genesis 40:4a)

While wrongfully imprisoned, Joseph served his fellow prisoners. Isn't this both beautiful and so very challenging? We are called to serve one another as well. Our future is contingent upon it!

Let's not leave Daniel out of the discussion today! He found himself in a foreign land, taken away from his family, had a Babylonian name change forced upon him, and placed in the palace of the king. He could have responded like many of us would have, "I refuse to be here. I have a destiny in God, and it does not include learning your language and receiving a foreign name. I refuse to serve." This knee-jerk response would have cost Daniel his destiny and, most likely, his life. But he chose the walk of humility and service. And he chose well. It was not long at all before he gained an audience with the king. The Bible actually says the king inquired of Daniel. He found him ten times better than all his magicians and astrologers.

Joseph always had the ability to rule in wisdom. Daniel always had the ability to interpret dreams and visions. However, it was not *until* both men were proven that the platform was present for them to come before kings. Service and humility were integral keys to swing that door wide open. I believe the enemy has some of us in a snare. We know we carry a call from God. We know our strengths and spiritual gifts. We are anxious to launch out and give the world what we have. But we've forgotten the most important part—CHARACTER! Gifts are, well, given freely, but gifts are not what we need to endure the call. Gifts open the door to the call, but character, Godly character, holds the door open. One of the most important character traits to be developed in us is *service*.

> *"Whosoever of you will be the chiefest* (first, best, foremost), *shall be servant of all" (Mark 10:44).*

Father, first of all, we repent of being pious and arrogant by leaving service for others to do. Lord, You are sounding an alarm for Your people to the importance of serving. Being a servant is getting dirty to make others clean. Jesus, You perfectly displayed this by washing the disciples' feet. And I believe they were really dirty. They left clean; You left dirty. This is exactly what You did on the cross. You became a servant to all by taking on the filthy, smelly sin of the entire human race. You took on my shame, my guilt, and my pain. And in turn, You gave me relationship with our Father. Because of You, I'm clean and free. I love You, Lord! I need the Holy Spirit's help to live this life of service. Remind me that the way UP is always DOWN. Help us…help me! In Jesus' name, I pray all things. Amen.

Saturday Jasper's Story

Your own ears will hear Him. Right behind you a voice will say, "This is the way you should go, whether to the right or to the left" (Isaiah 30:21, NLT)

Paul and I had our fourth child, Judah Benjamin, in February of 2010. We named him that because it means, "praising son at my right hand." Also, Benjamin was the youngest of Jacob's sons, and we *knew* Judah was our last. But for some reason, of which I cannot recall, I waited until December to schedule surgery to get my tube (I only had one) tied along with some other female surgery. The date was scheduled for the week of Christmas. I remember going in for my pre-operative visit six days before the surgery. The nurse at the doctor's office told me to go ahead over to the hospital where I work and get my blood work drawn. It was a Friday, but something in me said, "Just wait until Monday when you go to work to get your blood work." I knew this would not cause any disruption of the surgery, as the doctor would wait until the next week to look up my results anyway. I assumed that voice was my own. So on Monday, I got my blood work drawn while on my lunch break. Later in the day, after clocking out, I looked at my results. I was really curious about my hemoglobin more than anything. I knew I could not be pregnant as I was on birth control, so that result was of little interest to me...until I looked at it! The hCG level (pregnancy level) was 25 mlU/ml. This, my friends, is a positive pregnancy level. I just sat there and looked at the computer in shock. I was six days away from surgery and was finished having kids, but God had better plans. The phone conversation to my doctor's office was hilarious as the nurse just chuckled when I told her. The next day, I did a repeat test, and it had increased to 66 mlU/ml—a very healthy pregnancy indeed.

But, my friends, here's what you may not know. This level doubles every day the first twelve weeks of pregnancy. So on Monday it was 25, on Sunday 12, on Saturday 6, and on Friday (the day they told me to get it drawn) the hCG would have been **untraceable**. I would have continued through with the surgery plan and never known what I had lost. The female surgery would have been detrimental to the baby.

Lesson of the Day: Listen, listen, listen...God is speaking to you! His voice often sounds like your own. God is so close that sometimes it's hard to hear Him because He whispers. If I had not listened that day, well, I shudder to even think about what I might have lost.

Sunday Training to Trust:
A Purse, a Dryer, and Growth Spurts

*Ask and you shall receive, seek and you shall find, knock
and it shall be opened unto you* (Matthew 7:7)

The Purse: My first daughter, Kylie, came to me one time, crying. "Mommy, I lost my purse two weeks ago and have been afraid to tell you because it had money in it. I've looked everywhere."

After calming her down, I asked, "Kylie, does God know where your purse is?"

"Yes mam."

"Is He able to return it to you?"

"Yes mam."

I grabbed her hand and told her to repeat after me, "Lord, You know exactly where my purse is. I ask that You return it to me, and I believe You will. In Jesus' name. Amen."

I kid you not! When we said, "Amen," my phone rang. "Hello, is this Kylie?" I talked with a gentleman and discovered he had just, at that moment, sat down at a local restaurant we had eaten at two weeks prior. Her purse was in his booth, and he found my number written in her Bible. Here's what you don't know. At that restaurant, every night they pull out every booth to sweep and clean under the tables. We've seen them do it for years. There's no way a purse in one of their booths would have not been recognized for two weeks, unless God shielded it from their view until the moment our prayer was released. Kylie's faith soared that night. She knew God heard her and answered. It was quite supernatural indeed.

"I need a dryer": Being a family of seven, our washer and dryer are very important to us. One day, Paul called me into the laundry room. "April, pray over our dryer. It just died." I told him, "I don't feel led to, Buddy. I believe God has a better one for us." And I bebopped out of there, fully of joy, knowing God was doing something. I asked on social media if anyone was getting rid of a dryer. Five hours later, I was drying clothes again. Not only had someone given us a dryer, but *two* people had given us dryers—good ones—better than what I had! One of the wonderful people that gave that day drove over an hour to deliver it to me. They said they just had to help me. I had never even had one conversation with this person face-to-face! The other one who donated was a high school friend that I had not spoken to in twenty years.

Growth Spurts: I can't tell one story here because what I'm going to share has happened tens of times! When our kids hit growth spurts and run low on clothing, we have a tradition. The child and I stand in front of their closet, grab hands, and pray this prayer: "Lord, we have a need, and You promised to meet it. We ask for provision for clothing to be provided, and we celebrate now that it's done!" It's usually that week, if not the next day, that someone gives me a bag or multiple ones full of clothing of the exact size, season, and style that child has need of. And they are usually practically new as well!

Lesson of the Day: Bold faith receives bold rewards! God responds to faith, not need. Get courageous and audacious in your requests. He is a good Father and loves to give good gifts to His children!

Monday Jesus and Obedience

The past three weeks, the focus of this study has been on Old Testament biblical characters. We opened the study, week one, with Adam and Eve. Their act of sin cautions us even today. Through disobedience, they forfeited their earthly authority to the enemy. In the spiritual realm, an exchange occurred. We need to recall, and recall often, their story. May we be people of obedience to God! Week two, we learned about Joshua and some great characteristics that we can aspire to walk in. He was a man of courage and consecration. He wasn't afraid to lead people or to engage in warfare. And lastly, he was a man of praise. He understood the mighty weapon of praise that could be wielded against his enemy. Last week, we reviewed the stories of Joseph and Daniel and how they thrived in foreign lands. Although they were pulled out of a land familiar to them, they were able to walk in a *ruling* nature. Consequently, we can identify with them to a degree. We live in a land that has become a modern-day Egypt or Babylon with evil running rampant, but we, like these men, can thrive with the Lord in sight.

There are many intriguing men and women of the Bible that we can learn so much from. Some caution us with their mistakes, in turn, teaching us the importance of repentance if we do sin. Others spur us along with their extraordinary lives lived in full obedience to God. But there is one man who stands above rest. We can learn more from Him than anyone else in history. His name is Jesus. Can we just pause the study for a moment and audibly say that aloud together?

His name is Jesus!

There is power in that name. He is the image of the invisible God. Everything He did displayed the unseen Father perfectly. His life demonstrated the amazing balance of being seated with the Father and ruling on the earth over the enemy. The driving force of Christ's life was obedience to the Father. This is our highest calling in life, obedience to the Father! I want you to visualize a place. Its scenery is unmatched; its pleasures unparalleled. The peace that fills the air is tangible. Every need is met and every desire of heart granted as hearts delight in the Lord!

Delight thyself also in the Lord; and He shall give
thee the desires of thine heart (Psalm 37:4)

This is the close place of communion with the Father. The Son is always shining, the river is always flowing, and the song is forever being sung. What is this place? You ask. How can I live in a place like this? This destination is a *real* place, and the address is:

I WILL OBEY Avenue

Jesus lived with His feet on the soil of this land of the Earth. However, even as a child, He was about the Father's business. Later we encounter Jesus at the river asking to be baptized. This was an act of humility and obedience to the Father. Humility and obedience go hand in hand. Pride would not have allowed the Son of God to be dunked by a wild-haired, bug-eating John into the dirty Jordan River! But He *was* dunked. I marvel at what happened next. As He rose out of the water, the Father spoke from Heaven confirming the call upon His Son, and the Holy Spirit descended upon His life. It was not until *that* moment that Jesus began to preach the Kingdom of God and to flow in signs, healings, wonders, and miracles.

And Jesus, when He was baptized, went up straightway out of
the water; and, lo, the heavens were opened unto Him, and He
saw the Spirit of God descending like a dove, and lighting upon

Him; And lo a voice from heaven, saying, "This is my beloved
Son, in whom I am well pleased" (Matthew 3:16-17)

The lesson for us is that obedience to God brings the super-natural into our lives, and we need the supernatural to do the work of God! Do you remember in the Old Testament a man named Naaman? He was instructed by the prophet's servant to dip in the Jordan River to receive healing from his ailment. At first, he was so offended at the idea of getting in the dirty waters of the Jordan. To top it off, he was annoyed that the prophet himself did not come out to meet him with this instruction. Listen to the pride in his voice.

"I thought, He will surely come out to me, and stand, and call on
the name of the Lord his God, and strike his hand over the place,
and recover (me). Are not ... the rivers of Damascus, better than
all the waters of Israel? May I not wash in them, and be clean?"
So he turned and went away in a rage (2 Kings 5:11-12)

He later relented and dipped. He was made whole as he obeyed. Fast-forward to Jesus' day. He had no problem getting right into that river to be baptized—the same river, mind you! Maybe you identify yourself with Jesus, and you are diving into obedience headfirst. Or maybe you are like Naaman. You have found yourself hesitating to obey because it wasn't savory to do so. But even though Naaman pondered disobeying, he ended up in that water. I want to speak hope to someone today who has hesitated in obeying the Lord. On the other side of that act of humble obedience could be the greatest miracle you've ever known. I've just today made a step of obedience that would make no sense to any man, but I know that I will see the hand of God move in my life because of it. As the tears stream down my cheeks even now, I know there's never been anyone who regretted obeying the Father!

9

Father, give us the desire to obey You. We want to be like trees planted by rivers of water. But we know that our roots will only go as deep as our obedience. Jesus was the fulfillment of a life lived in obedience to You. God, I speak over each of us an increase in hunger to obey. For those in obedience, let them see the supernatural open up before their eyes. For those who have hesitated, there is no condemnation, but there is a challenge to move forward. Lord, I declare that all is not lost, and You are well able to restore all the years of our disobedience. We love You and receive love from You. In Jesus' name, we pray. Amen.

Tuesday Jesus the Provider

When Jesus was born, purpose was born! He came into the earth to accomplish a multilayered mission. That mission included: salvation, redemption, healing, miracles, deliverance, and restoration. Studying His life is like reading a how-to book on "ruling on the earth" and being "seated in the clouds." His life was perfectly balanced between time spent *above* in prayer and time spent *below* ruining the devil's day! I love to read the accounts of His supernatural power on display. He raised the dead, healed the blind, and returned sanity to the deranged of mind. But today the Holy Spirit impressed upon my heart the way in which the Lord met needs during His three years of ministry. He fed people, called forth a coin from a fish's mouth to pay taxes, multiplied fish in the nets, and washed dirty feet. Not only did He minister to the spirit of man, but He also met their physical needs.

Jesus' first miracle was performed to meet a need. No one was sick or hungry. No one needed raising from the dead. The crisis of need that Jesus met was empty wine vats at a wedding. Don't you find it interesting that the launching of Jesus' miracle campaign started by turning water into wine? The amazing narrative of this event is found in John 2.

> *And the mother of Jesus was there: And both Jesus was called, and His disciples, to the marriage. And when they wanted wine, (Mary) saith unto Him, "They have no wine." Jesus saith unto her, "Woman, what have I to do with thee? Mine hour (season) is not yet come." His mother saith unto the servants, "Whatsoever He saith unto you, do"* (John 2:1b-5)

In reading the above text, my mind pictures Mary in attendance at the wedding, but Jesus and His followers being *called* to come. It's as if Jesus' presence at the wedding had purpose...and it did! He was not *just* another attendee. Then we hear the conversation between Jesus and Mary. Jesus' response to her request for help is so revealing of the mother-son relationship between Mary and Him. Can you hear the perplexed tone in Jesus' voice? *"Mine hour is not yet come."* But look at Mary's response! She just goes right on and calls for the servants. We can learn a lot about faith from her! In this story, John pulls back the veil on the humanity of Jesus. Jesus knew His season for miracle working was soon approaching but had not yet arrived. However, there was a need present, and someone, aka Momma, was interceding on behalf of the people. And did Jesus ever meet the need! He would not reject her plea of faith. He instructed the servants to fill **six water pots of stone** with water, and they did...to the brim.

The number 6, a jar or vessel, and stone all represent humanity. We are the vessels He wishes to fill with new wine![*10]

Then He simply told them to dip out of the water and give it to the governor, also known as the director of entertainment. By the time the ladle met the governor's mouth, new wine was present for the tasting.

And saith unto him, "Every man at the beginning doth set forth good wine; and when men have well drunk, then that which is worse: but thou hast kept the good wine until now" (John 2:10)

Let's examine this story more closely to glean what we can for our own lives. Jesus knew His time for public notoriety had not come, yet His mother stepped out in faith by telling the servants to obey Him. He would not publicly disgrace her or disobey God by bringing attention to Himself yet, so He, in His perfect wisdom, performed His first miracle under the radar! I do not know your perception of this story up until this time, but I've always thought the whole wedding party knew what Jesus did. But they did not. Read the story! Don't you love learning from Holy Spirit!?

And the master of the banquet tasted the water that had been turned into wine. He did not realize where it had come from, though the servants who had drawn the water knew... (John 2:9a, NIV)

The only people privy to the supernatural occurrence that day were *servants*. Isn't this amazing? The same Jesus that performed miracles before the eyes of the people, the Pharisees, the tax collectors, etc., performed His first for the eyes of servants alone. As we are obedient, we get to see His power where others might miss it. He met a need but did not need to be seen doing it! He blessed people, the wedding goers, and they never knew it was Him.

Let's yearn to be like Jesus! When we meet others' needs quietly, things shift in our lives. This is a timely and specific word for many readers today! Go about your day and look for empty wine vats! People are in need all around you, and there are *Marys* crying out on their behalf. If it is in your capacity to meet a need and attribute all glory to God, do it! May we disappear into the wedding crowd as they drink the wine of the Lord that we have the privilege to usher in!

---

*Oh, Father, I'm in love with this Word today! I thank You for revelation that only the Holy Spirit can offer. Make us like Jesus. Until our season comes, as we wait, give us **courage to be hidden**! And then when the time comes, give us courage to be seen. Give us such love for the people that we **have** to meet their need in Your name! Lord, may our lives forever point to Your Son! We are in awe of the beautiful humility, obedience, and sacrifice in which His life was lived out. We want that life for us. Grant it. I pray in Jesus' name! Amen.*

Wednesday Title Versus Authority

11

For He taught them as one having authority, and not as the scribes (Matthew 7:29)

Authority as defined by *Webster*:

- The power to give orders or make decisions
- The power and right to direct or control someone or something
- The confident quality of someone who knows a lot about something or who is respected or obeyed by others[12]

Authority as defined by *Strong's Concordance* #G1849:

- Privilege
- Possessing a force, capacity, competency, freedom, or mastery
- A magistrate
- Superhuman

- Delegated influence
- Jurisdiction, liberty, power, right, or strength[13]

Today the Holy Spirit has been speaking to me about authority versus title. We as a family were watching *The Andy Griffin Show*, and I saw a great scene that I'd like to share for illustrative purposes. Andy is asked by Aunt Bea to help a gentleman by letting him work at the courthouse. The man is thrilled to get to work so closely to Sheriff Andy. While Andy is away tending to matters, the man puts on Barney's deputy uniform and badge. He then journeys out and soon comes upon a brawl of two men. The men are tussling back and forth with a crowd surrounding them.

He keeps shouting, "I have a badge! I have a badge!" But no one takes note of his presence. He is all but invisible to them. In steps Andy, the long-standing sheriff of Mayberry, well-respected and honored by his townspeople. Andy simply shouts, "Knock it off!" And the brawl is over as soon as it began. (Ross & Ruskin, 1965)

As soon as the scene ended, I was reminded of the story in Acts 19 when some wannabe deputies, also known as the Sons of Sceva, tried to cast out an evil spirit. The result was very startling for them.

And the evil spirit answered and said, "Jesus I know,
and Paul I know; by who are ye?" (Acts 19:15)

What happens next is just as unsettling. The man, who had the evil spirit, whooped up on all seven of these men and left them naked and wounded. I feel a great calling to inform some and remind others about the authority of the kingdom. It is only through relationship with Jesus that we are able to enact this authority. Otherwise, we are carrying a shiny title with no power to back it up. Remember this very important fact, the demons know who is real and who is not. Someone can approach the enemy by saying all the right things, "In Jesus' name, I rebuke you and cast you out of my life." But their response will be tied to more than our saying the syllables "Je-sus." I am not taking away from the sacredness of His name. I love His name; I love to hear it and say it. But I'm afraid our culture doesn't realize what *name* means. As I stated before, it is so much more than pronounced syllables.

According to *Strong's*, the word *name* translates to authority *and* character.[14]

I often teach and speak about the importance of our position in Christ, but I have become aware that I need to go deeper in teaching about walking in the *name* of Jesus. As we see above, *name* means authority *and* character. We cannot wield His name as a tagline in prayer or a shotgun blast at the enemy. We must see that invoking His name is synonymous with operating under His authority. One cannot walk in Jesus' authority without being endowed with His power.

Remember what we discussed earlier about the television show? The man in the uniform might have been in costume. He had the badge, he used the title, he spoke with confidence, but he was not backed by the power from above. Look back to our opening text! Jesus spoke with power and not like the scribes. *Scribe* was a very desirable title in Jesus' day, yet there was no power behind their words. A title means nothing in the spiritual realm, but authority means everything. It's both our personal relationship with Jesus *and* our walking in His character that empower us to wield His authority! This is huge God's people! It is only through close connection to Jesus that His character is developed in us.

But we all, with open face beholding as in a mirror the glory of the Lord, are changed into the same image from glory to glory, even as by the Spirit of the Lord (2 Corinthians 3:18)

It is only in His presence that we are transformed into His image, otherwise known as His character. I urge each of us today to increase our time and attention in His presence. Reading the Word, worship, praise, and prayer are all aspects of entering into this place, but I challenge us to spend time waiting in holy silence before Him. There is a beauty that is released as we quiet our minds and *see* Him. We are changed in those moments. Let's pray *in the name*, let's walk *in the name*, and let's rule *in the name* of Jesus! He is our husband that has gone away but has said, "Act in my stead while I'm away and use my name at will." May we honor Him in that way.

Father, we come to You in the authority and character of Jesus! We don't want recognition of man. Therein lies the lie that we can be important because of a title. Lord, what we desire is to be recognized by the invisible world instead. We want the ability in Christ to walk in victory over our enemy. And God we have learned that only comes through relationship with You. Bring our hearts closer to Yours. Take our preoccupied minds away from the clutter of life and quiet us at Your side. We want to be changed into the image of Your Son. We want to look like Him, speak like Him, and act like Him. You share that desire with us. He is the firstborn of many sons. A great mold was cast with His life. Help us Holy Spirit to live out our days pleasing the Father. In Jesus' name (authority, and character), we pray. Amen.

Thursday Secrets to the Supernatural: Knowing Him

And in the morning, rising up a great while before day, he went out, and departed into a solitary place, and there prayed (Mark 1:35)

Prayer is so important in any Christian's life. It is literally *being* with the Father! Jesus understood this and responded to the call to draw away and pray. We see in Mark 1 Jesus stepping into His earthly ministry. So much happens in this chapter. I highly recommend reading it in its entirety. Jesus was baptized in verse 9. In verse 13, He was driven into the wilderness for forty days by the Spirit of God to endure temptation from Satan. Upon leaving the wilderness, Jesus immediately begins: preaching the Kingdom of God, calling disciples to His side, teaching in the synagogue, casting out demons, amazing the crowd with His authority, rebuking fevers, and healing sicknesses. His fame spread so wide that in Mark 1:33, all the city was gathered together at the door as He worked miracles. I don't know about you, but I desire to do everything Jesus did! I know this is promised to me as a believer.

"Verily, verily (repeated to indicate He means what He's about to say), I say unto you, He that believeth on me, the works that I do shall he do also; and greater works than these shall he do; because I go unto my Father" (John 14:12)

The first objective of today's devotion is to prove by the Word that you are called to flow in the supernatural. The second objective is to reveal the secret behind obtaining this power.

I want to smash all the lies of the enemy concerning the call upon you...yes, you! You are just as called to live like Jesus did, as anyone else. You've prayed before and not seen results. You've shared with others and not seen the reaction you had hoped for. You've watched tragedy unfold and heard the lies of the enemy that you cannot make an impact. And alone you can't! But the Holy Spirit *in you* can! Even Jesus did not perform one miracle until the Holy Spirit descended upon Him at His baptism. I believe the church is longing to see the *real* demonstrated. I believe the world is looking for the same. And they are waiting on this power to flow through *you*!

> *"And my speech and my preaching was not with enticing words of man's wisdom, but in demonstration of the Spirit and of power"* (Paul, the Apostle) (1 Corinthians 2:4)

The above verse blows away the lie that you need to know more, speak better, or go through self-help before you minister. Lies, lies, all lies! There *is* something that *must* occur in you to be fit for ministry, but it does not include self-improvement at all. It involves self-denial! We can agree with the enemy that we are not worthy, but we do not turn our deficiency into a campaign for *self-help*. No! Rather we turn our frailty toward a relationship with the Lord. We do not look inward to ourselves. We die to ourselves and then can be filled with Him. He is what people need. He is the Healer! He is the Deliverer! He is the Savior! Spoiler alert: if you want to flow in miracles, get a hold of Him! He must be the only prize we run toward. I love the fact that Paul, previously called Saul, was the wisest of the wise before his conversion. He was the Pharisee of Pharisees, knowing their traditions through and through. But look what Paul says below. Paul realized that he could not help anyone apart from God's power.

> *"I count all things as loss for the excellency of the knowledge of Christ Jesus my Lord: for whom I have suffered the loss of all things, and do count them as dung, that I may win Christ"* (Philippians 3:8)

Paul knew that the knowledge of our Jesus was the greatest of all to be gained. An empowering occurs when one denies everything else and leans their trust weight on Jesus. That, my friend, is *miracle* territory. When we put no stock in our assets. When our eyes are locked on Jesus, *ministry* disappears. What do I mean by this? Many of us, on-fire people for God, want so desperately to minister and flow in miracles, and rightfully so! However, I want to encourage each of us to take our eyes, our gaze, off of *anything* but Jesus. The verse above shows an amazing transfer where Paul counts all lost so that he may win Christ. May we lose sight of ministry, healing, preaching, and everything else and have laser focus on Christ and Him alone. The amazing thing that occurs when we find Christ is we receive everything else relating to His kingdom. We will preach without trying and win the lost without striving. He will do it all through us! But if we are seeking anything, but simply Him, we've missed it all! Success in the kingdom is not measured by any outcome except for knowing Him! I never want to hear Him say these words to me: *"I never **knew** you: depart from me, ye that work iniquity."* (Matthew 7:23)

On that fateful day, no one will hear, "You didn't get enough souls saved," "You didn't memorize enough verses," or "You didn't preach enough." According to the above verse, knowing Him and being known by Him will be the focus of it all. *That* is the secret! The reason Jesus flowed in miracles, preached in power, and was obedient to the call was because He *knew* the Father. This knowing is more than an awareness of the other person. It is an intimate knowledge that only comes through spending time together. May we follow in Jesus' footsteps and get to know the Lord today!

Father, simply put, we want to know You and be known by You. May our thoughts and attention turn from everything else, even the good stuff, to You. You're the goal! You're the prize! You're the mark! Lord, we want Your presence in our lives. We love the gifts You give. We love healing, power, ministry, and miracles. But we love You more! May we never get skewed to focusing on anything more than You. From the moment we look away from You, Your image gets blurry in our sight, and we start to sink. But like Peter, when that occurs, please pull us up. Show us mercy for we are truly in need of it. Thank You, God. It's in Jesus' name we pray. Amen.

Friday Secrets to the Supernatural: Don't Miss Out Looking for the Spectacular!

Supernatural as defined by *Webster*:

- of or relating to an order of existence beyond the visible observable universe[15]

According to the above definition, *supernatural* is anything relating to the unseen world. Therefore, every encounter with the Lord is supernatural! Salvation is supernatural. Prayer is supernatural. I believe many times we miss the *supernatural* in search for the *spectacular*. Yes, there are moments of jaw-dropping occurrences, and oh let there be more! I have had the privilege of seeing visible healings occur in an instant! I've watched people with knee pain, hobbling around, after prayer have no pain at all. I've watched as a lady jumped up and down after prayer because her pain was gone. Her response was, "Oooh, pray for my kidneys too!" Her faith was soaring after feeling a tangible touch from the Lord. I watched a skin condition vanish off my daughter after tormenting her for five years. I love the spectacular! Do not get me wrong. However, I want to bring awareness to the simple supernatural occurrences that we too often overlook.

I had a beautiful moment with my daughters this week. I believe this will illustrate the simplicity of the supernatural. The three of us were seated around a table discussing the Word of God. I felt the Holy Spirit nudging me to teach them how to wait upon the Lord in prayer.

But they that wait upon the Lord shall renew their strength;
they shall mount up with wings as eagles; they shall run, and
not be weary, they shall walk, and not faint (Isaiah 40:31)

I instructed them, eleven and seven years old, that Mommy was going to set a timer for two minutes and that we were going to meditate on the Lord together. They love new adventures, so they were all in. I had them close their eyes, think about Jesus, and just listen. I reminded them that God moves upon faith and to believe that God *would* speak to them. I encouraged them to pay attention to what went through their mind or imagination as we quietly worshipped. I was astounded at the mighty presence of God that *immediately* poured into that dining room. The stillness was so peaceful. As soon as the timer went off, my youngest daughter, Bella, ran to her room. I didn't know if she had been bored or why she left the room, but she came running back with pencil and paper.

"Momma, I want to draw what I saw," she said joyfully. And then she proceeded to draw a picture of lightning bolts with what she called *sprinkles* coming down from them. "Momma, I saw bright light, and it was letting sprinkles come down, full of joy. I was running into it and bringing other people with me."

You guessed it! I was in tears. My other daughter said, "I did not see anything in my head but heard the song 'Fill Me Up, God,'" and she began scribbling a picture of an open box. I stopped her right there. "Kylie, you are not drawing that open box for no reason. The Lord's leading and voice often sounds like your own voice."

This is a great lesson for us all in hearing the voice of God. Think about it. Who gave you an imagination…the enemy? No! The Lord told Adam to name the animals. He allows and *encourages* our creativity. He speaks in any way we can believe for. Let's step out in faith and believe that God is really here, really speaking, and really listening to us. Is that such a crazy thought!? Okay, let's get back to the kitchen table. The girls enjoyed this so much they had us do it again…twice. The second time the young one starting drawing before the timer was even done! She said she saw the blood of Jesus coming down from Heaven and she ran into it, but a lot of others were running away from it. During this exercise, the Holy Spirit reminded me that supernatural events occur all day long but are often missed because we are looking for something bigger.

Bella's first prophetic sketch at eight years old!

I believe it's those who cherish these alone times with God who get to experience the public displays of His power as well. Just as Jesus' first miracle of turning water in wine was unseen, our starting point begins in private as well. **A true heart is always developed in private.**

The Lord plants supernatural, invisible seeds into our heart each time He speaks to us. I know, for me, He confirms words over and over again. I used to get so excited that I would run out and tell everyone. I wanted to share with others everything I had heard. Many times I faced disappointment, as their response did not match mine. The Lord spoke so clearly to me and said, "I put these seeds into your heart for you to meditate on and inquire of me about. It is *your* seed specifically designed for you and your destiny. I want this seed to go down deep in your heart and spring up. From that sprig, a tree will develop and eventually produce fruit. It will be *that* fruit others can eat of. But stop giving away *your* seed."

The revelation hit me between the eyes that I had been giving away my seed! What I came to realize was that God wants to have *private* conversations with each of us. He wants to tell us secrets. He wants to plant supernatural seeds. Remember Mary, when the seed of Jesus came to her womb, didn't go about sharing with everyone publicly.

> *But Mary **kept** all these things, and pon-*
> *dered them in her heart* (Luke 2:19)

Why is this so important for us? First of all, the Lord intrigues us with these revelations to seek His counsel. He seeks relationship above all else. Secondly, instead of going to everyone else for confirmation or clarity, He wants us to learn *His* voice. I believe this is a huge component of seeing miraculous occurrences in the public arena. If we do not have dependence on Him for our security when *seen* miracles come, we will respond in the wrong way. We will find our value in the miracle or in others' responses instead of in Him. And then when we pray and nothing happens, we will collapse in failure.

> The outcome of prayers do not determine our suc-
> cess. Our obedience to God does!

We need to get to the place that praying for the sick is easy because we walk so closely to Him. To the extent, we encounter the supernatural presence of God in our prayer closets, we will encounter His supernatural power publicly.

If you are interested in seeing the book of Acts come to life before your eyes, run to the secret place! See every encounter with Him as supernatural. Allow Him to speak through your imagination; He is the one who gave it to you! Wake up in the morning looking for divine moments that no one else would even recognize. Get alone, get quiet, and listen.

Father, we want to see people made whole, saved, and delivered. But help us to stop skipping steps. Open our eyes to see the supernatural right in front of us. Lord, I'm reminded of the saying, "Be thankful for what you have before asking for more." May we begin to thank You for these sacred moments now believing that seeds are going deep into our hearts. God, let not one seed go dormant again! I pray we will stop seeking anything from man that only You can give. You give assurance! You give confirmation! You give hope! Grow us up beyond trying to impress anyone. I thank You for allowing us the privilege to approach You each day. Help us to see You put the super on our natural. We love you. In Jesus' name we pray. Amen.

Saturday Deb's Story

(photo and story approved by D. Cox for use)

"Behold, I give unto you power to tread on serpents and scorpions, and over all the power of the enemy…" (Luke 10:18b)

During a season when I taught a ladies' Bible study, something amazing happened I'd like to share. We met together every week. Twice a month our meetings were purely Bible discussion, and the other two meetings were prayer meetings. And the prayer meetings were not your normal prayer meetings; instead, God told me to teach these ladies to pray through demonstration. We would gather in the prayer room and begin with worship. Then as the Holy Spirit led, we would begin praying for one another or for specific needs. As we lifted up needs, I would teach about biblical models of prayer and how to do it effectively. We would all take part in praying. On one of these prayer days, Ms. Deb asked for prayer. The enemy had been battling her heavy with depression. We gathered around her and began to pray. Keep in mind she has not only given me permission to share but has also encouraged me to share her story of freedom! As we began to pray, her eyes closed, and she sat back in the chair. She became only what I can describe as unresponsive. We began to rebuke and bind the Spirit of Depression and cast it out of her mind and life. At one point, I stepped back and looked as these fiery women of God prayed with such compassion over our sweet sister. I used this as an opportunity and talked the ladies through this process of deliverance. I watched each woman rise up with boldness, commanding the release of Deb from the enemy's lies. Eventually and not without a fight, the enemy let go, and we knew that spirit had lifted. Deb opened her eyes and was a bit stunned. "What all just happened?", she asked. I told her she was free of that spirit. Her face and especially her eyes lit up with, well, life! She looked like a new woman.

But then something so amazing happened that still makes me smile! She began raising her right arm above her head. She began to rejoice, saying, "My arm doesn't hurt anymore. My shoulder doesn't hurt." Through the power of God, depression lifted, and Deb was healed in the process. All this took about fifteen minutes, and boy it was well worth the time. There's nothing better than looking on the sweet face of someone set free by the power of God working through us.

Lesson of the Day: Through Christ, you've been given power over the enemy. What are you doing with that power?

Sunday The Rewards of Delighting

Delight thyself also in the Lord; and He shall give you
the desires of your thine heart (Psalm 37:4)

In the year 2014, the Lord taught me so much about delighting in Him. It seems like every time I went to prayer or worship I would just delight in Him. I don't remember asking for a whole bunch, or even thinking about myself while I spent time with Him. It was a beautiful season of delighting. I remember looking up toward Heaven all the time and just smiling. I wanted above all to delight in His Presence. During this season, I had such joy and peace that I had not previously encountered. It was as if my eyes were opened wider than before.

I began having a strong compelling to become creative. This was not my forte, as my natural character is type A, black and white, and very linear. But the urge would not resolve. I found myself at Walmart buying paint and canvases. It made no sense I did not paint, draw, or have any artistic ability, but I wanted to paint…and paint I did! That night I locked myself in my bathroom (remember I have five kids), put on worship music, and began to paint. I spent hours in there and felt like I was discovering a whole new April. And the talent immediately flowed as you can see in the first picture above. Okay, so hopefully you can hear the silliness in my tone. It looked awful and did not even make sense. But I was so fulfilled and had a blast. Something in my brain was unlocking.

For months to follow, I kept painting in my spare time, and even took up sketching (something I told myself I never could do) and poetry. During the next year, I began to improve and learn new techniques. The Lord then began to reveal to me what was happening. When I was a child in first grade, I wanted so desperately to be artistic. My teacher at that time made a negative comment one day that completely shut me down. My confidence was shot, and I settled in my heart I would never be able to make beautiful art. This was a memory I had, totally forgotten. When God reminded me of it, He told me the plan of the enemy was to steal from me this desire as a young child. But when I began delighting in the Lord, God was in covenant with His word, according to Psalm 37:4, to "give me the desires of my heart"…desires I had forgotten I ever had! How incredible is that? The cool thing is the second painting was complete one year to the month of the first one, and it was painted over the first! I have been privileged to sell multiple pieces of art. That is something I never thought could have happened, but delighting in the Lord was the key to unlock this buried treasure in my heart. What has been buried in your heart that needs to come back out?

Lesson of the Day: Delight in Him. He is the resurrector of dreams long died!

Poem: Salvation

SALVATION

My hearing is weak,
but Your speaking is
strong.
My patience is thin,
but Yours just goes on.
My mind is scattered,
Yours has me
enamored.
My resolve is frail,
but You took the nails.
My love meets its end,
but Yours always
wins.
My vision is near,
but You see every fear.
So in my shame,
I call out Your name.
Over all my
weaknesses,
Your voice now
proclaims,

To "Lean on me,
the source of it all.
Come through me,
I AM your Entrance Hall,
To access the Father
and His delight.
To be at His throne,
and dance in His sight.
But you cannot come
to this place on your own.
For your sins are too great,
and your guilt far too strong.
So step through my blood,
and come by my grace.
For once you arrive,
healing's found in this place.
So take my strength
to carry you on.
And hold my hand
For, now, your sin is gone."

I respond, "Yes,
Yes my Lord,
I will follow,
And surrender my
hurt,
all my sorrow,
And I'll trade all
my weakness,
for Your every
strength,
And I'll never look
back,
keeping sin at
arm's length.
I cherish Your
cross,
I cherish Your
blood,
I cherish Your
salvation,
I've been pulled
from the mud.
So I give my all
to You this day.
You are the The
life,
The Truth,
And, Yes, You are
my Way."

April Babb
#peopleablaze

96

Sketches and Paintings

Cornerstone

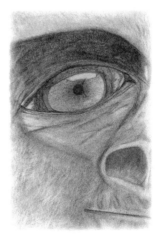

Beloved

Delight

Strength & Wonder

Lion of Warfare-Judah

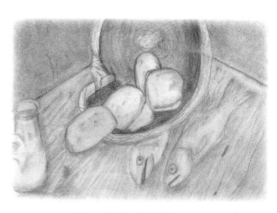

Lunch for 5,000

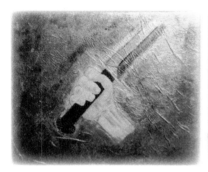

Armed with the Word

Joy

Bloom

Rest

New Day

Provision

Idea from awalker010.deviantart.com
Drawn by A. Babb

Set a Fire

Shelter   **Reliance**

Breaking Night   **You are the Flame**

Monday Secrets to the Supernatural: Lessons from the Beloved

Part 1/2

We too many times pursue the *works* of Christ instead of simply pursuing the *wonder* of Christ. Let's examine the life of a New Testament character that lived in the wonder of Jesus. When others ran in fear, he stood with supernatural courage. When others focused on temporal things, his sight was on the eternal. He is often neglected in discussion in lieu of others that lived *louder* lives, such as John the Baptist, Peter, or Paul. The man of whom I am speaking is none other than John, the disciple.

Meditating on John has offered some amazing insights I'd like to share with you. I will be contrasting his life against Peter's for the sake of comparison. Both were powerhouses for the kingdom. They had the same access to Jesus. Both were pillars for the early church. However, there is a difference that is fascinating and contains a pivotal lesson for many of us. I hope for us all to catch the vision that John had as the *Beloved*. In understanding this, we can begin to walk in the supernatural with ease!

Peter was bold from the beginning. Jesus simply passed by and said, "Follow me," and Peter immediately obeyed. Leaving all he had known was of no consequence to him. He valued being with Christ above staying in the familiar. This was quite courageous! We remember from Matthew 16:16 that Peter was the one who identified Jesus as the "Christ, the Son of the living God." Surely Peter was called and blessed by God to lead.

However, Peter's life also demonstrates pitfalls for us to avoid. When the heat was on, Peter was fickle and got off track. Jesus' time to suffer was drawing near. He began to share details of His death with the disciples when Peter rebuked him. But Jesus returned the rebuke and said, "Get thee behind me, Satan" (Matthew 16:23). Peter disappoints once more when Jesus asks him to stay awake and pray. He was found asleep not once but three times. Jesus knew the importance of Peter's need to pray. The temptation to deny Christ would soon come. Sadly it did come. And Peter did fall…miserably. He denied Christ three times and then ran away in fear and shame. At the cross, he was nowhere to be found. In looking at the lives of these men, there are distinctive differences. John did not seem to appreciate the fanfare like Peter. He was a quiet but steady fixture throughout the Gospels. In John's epistle, he repeatedly identified himself as the "disciple Jesus loved."

*Now there was **leaning** on Jesus' bosom one of His disciples, whom Jesus loved* (John 13:23)

The disciple Jesus loved

Embedded in the above four words is the secret to John's success. Time and time again, we see Peter declaring his love and allegiance for Jesus. He constantly attempted to prove his love and trust for Jesus, many times to no avail. He had a knack for sticking his foot in his mouth. At one point when beholding Jesus glorified with Moses and Elijah, he suggested building a tabernacle for each. This did not go over well. He asks Jesus to call him out on the water and soon began to sink as fear took over. He first forbade Jesus to wash his feet and then in the next breath asked Jesus to wash his whole person. In the climax of Peter's story, he pledges:

"Though all shall be offended because of thee, yet will I never be offended" (Matthew 26:33)

I can almost hear the rooster crow as I reflect on this pledge. Although this season in Peter's life was very dark, the Lord offered redemption and restoration. Peter was later filled with the Holy Spirit and was forever changed to never again deny Christ. It ended up costing him his own life as a martyr, and for that we honor him. However, let's learn from his pre-cross mistakes so that we can avoid the same snares Peter faced.

Peter's whole identity was focused on *his* ability to love and serve God. This is an error that we cannot afford. If we believe that we will flow in the supernatural because of some great quality in *us*, we will soon hear the rooster crow too!

The rock beneath our feet can never have our name on it!

Peter was commended only when he stated the supremacy of Christ. It was after his profession of Jesus as the Christ, the Son of the living God that Jesus called Peter a rock. It was the *understanding* of Jesus' stability that earned Peter the new name, not any *action* on his part. Just a few verses later, we see Jesus' stern rebuke toward Peter when he forbids that Jesus would have to suffer. These were the words of Satan coming through Peter. This serves as a caution for us. Thinking we can function apart from the Lord is a setup for disaster. And it is easier to do than we think. All that is required for this failure is leaning on our own understanding and strength.

Jesus turned and said to Peter, "Get behind me, Satan! You are a stumbling block to Me; you do not have in mind the concerns of God, but merely human concerns." (Matthew 16:28, NIV)

---

*Father, thank You for Your Word and all it teaches us! We desire to read and see more than we have before. Holy Spirit, open our eyes to see **ourselves** on the pages. Help us to see things in us when we read of these biblical characters and adjust accordingly. Set us free from the mindset that our actions amount to anything apart from Your revelation. Flush us of all pride. Jesus, You are the **Rock** beneath us, and You are never shaken! We love You and keep our eyes focused on You. In Jesus' name we pray. Amen.*

Tuesday Secrets to the Supernatural: Lessons from the Beloved

Part 2/2

Peter had zeal. Peter had boldness. But Peter had pride. Pride must not be present in a disciple of Jesus. Our own merits will always fail and fall under pressure. One day we will be sky-high because someone was healed, and the next day we will find our self in a pit because they were not. This is a roller coaster we cannot ride. Only the Lord's faithfulness is never-changing; therefore, He has to be our focus! Peter's all-in-all was built on a flimsy foundation—that being himself and his own loyalty to Christ. He constantly declared his devotion to Jesus, but his actions did not back that up.

John lived a different way. His desired place was not one of prominence but at the bosom of Jesus. His strength was in Christ alone. It is a beautiful thing when one awakens to their identity—as the *disciple that Jesus loves*. When Jesus was enduring the most painful moment of His life, John was there. Jesus looked down from the cross and *saw* John. John was steady because the rock beneath His feet was called "Jesus loves me." Therefore, he had nothing to fear the day of the crucifixion. Others ran and hid, but he was there, *still there*, at the feet of His savior worshipping with his tears. How lovely, how marvelous the love that Jesus has for us is! It will allow us to stand unafraid in the most grave of situations as we keep our eyes on Him. So what if they captured John? He had Jesus' love! In fact, look at what it meant to Jesus to have John there!

Then saith He (Jesus) to the disciple, "Behold thy mother!" And from that hour that disciple took her unto his own home (John 19:27)

Jesus gave John His mother!

Those that remain close to Jesus will receive things that are close to His heart this same way! What an awesome privilege that was! After Jesus' resurrection, He appeared on the shore. The disciples went back to what they knew, fishing. Isn't it interesting that John was the first to recognize him?

*That disciple whom Jesus loved saith unto
Peter, "It is the Lord" (John 21:7)*

Fast-forward to the book of Acts. The disciples are facing immense persecution, and even executions. Eleven of the twelve are martyred. Guess who survived? John was the lone survivor of the group. I find this fascinating! I like to think that because John saw Jesus' suffering on the cross, he had already endured the greatest pain one could. John faced the execution of Christ and did not have to face his own. According to historians, John did face an attempt on his life but survived it! After that didn't work, they exiled him to an island called Patmos, and the rest is history…well, Revelation actually! It was there that he had the privilege of seeing Jesus like no one else was able to—as Alpha and Omega. Think about it! The King of kings and Lord of lords, the Lion of the tribe of Judah, chose to reveal Himself to the disciple who knew how loved he was. Others knew him as the Word of God, as the Lamb of God, but *only* John had the supernatural revelation of Him as returning King! Wow!

Let's be like John, who chose the identity of *Beloved* over any other name. As we lean fully on Jesus' love for us and not ours for Him, we will see Him reigning as our King and our Lord! We will see Him displayed in supernatural ways. Yes, we love him! Yes, we will give our lives for Him. But our *rock*, our *hope*, our *banner* is **He loves us**! Our name has become *Beloved*. Knowing He loves us provides a boldness that comes no other way. It is those that know they are loved that turn the world upside down! Let's march forward fearlessly in His love for us.

---

*Father, oh, how You love us! We look to the cross and see the most amazing expression of love that has ever been displayed. There can be no doubt that You love us. May we stop trying to prove anything and rest against Your bosom. We will fail, we will mess up, but our stability is in You! Help us to be developed into people with Peter's **boldness** and John's **dependence**. God, give us perfect balance. We love You, but You love us more, and we celebrate that! In Jesus' name we pray. Amen.*

Wednesday Secrets to the Supernatural: Breaking the Lies

Not Now, Not Me

For every truth God has, you can be sure the enemy has a well-crafted lie to combat it. God speaks that we are to live obediently to His call. The enemy says, "Do what you want, and grace will cover it all." The Lord commands us to be filled with Holy Spirit. The enemy whispers that this is optional. The Lord shows repeatedly throughout the New Testament that miracles, signs, wonders, deliverances, healings, and salvations are signs that the Kingdom has come; but the enemy has deceived so many to believe these occurrences are unnecessary and impossible. The enemy is very smart. He knows how to bend the Word of God to meet his purposes. For example, I've heard it said before, "I haven't felt God in twenty years or ever seen a physical healing, but I don't need all that. I have faith." This is perversion and actually an excuse of why the person does not walk in the power of the Holy Spirit. Too many ignore Jesus' words in Mark 16:17-18.

*"And these **signs** shall **follow** them that believe..."*

I just hear the Lord saying, "Enough excuses." The church's calling is quite well-defined in this Mark passage. Our commission from Jesus is as follows: go, preach, baptize, cast out the enemy, allow the Holy Spirit to have His way in your lives, walk in authority over creeping things, walk in protection, and heal the sick in Jesus' authority.

A person can know the Word without knowing the *Word*. What do I mean? There is a book called the Word, aka the Bible, and then there's a person called the *Word*. The goal is to know the person and be known by Him. On the Day of Judgment, to the lost ones, He won't say, "You did not know enough Bible verses, depart from me." No, instead His departing words will be, "I never knew you." I look at it like this. Reading the Word tells me all about Jesus. It describes Him in every detail. It's like a portrait of who He is. But spending time with the *Word* Himself is like sitting back in a mold that is His image and becoming like Him. The Bible describes the mold, but spending time in His presence pushes me down into the mold to become like Him.

> *But we all, with open face beholding as in a glass the*
> *glory of the Lord, are changed into the same image*
> *from glory to glory.* (2 Corinthians 3:18a)

The Word (Bible) should lead us to an encounter with the Word Jesus![16]

Knowing the Bible, I can assure you of few things with confidence. Those that know Jesus and His Word intimately *will* feel something, and often. They *will* see healings. They *will* see deliverance and salvation occur before their eyes! Instead of making excuses of why we aren't seeing the works of Jesus in our lives, let's begin to shift our hearts to expectation. Maybe we have believed the lie that this supernatural *stuff* isn't for today. Or perhaps, we believe it is for today but just not for us. Someone else is more qualified and less fearful, so they can do it. Lies! Whatever lie Satan has baited your hook with, don't bite! If there is any deficit in our lives, it is *not* God's doing. I am not condoning self-condemnation or a works mentality! What I'm encouraging is self-evaluation. May we allow the light of the Lord to show us areas of our lives that hinder His supernatural power from flowing. The closer we get to Jesus, the more we begin to look like Him, and His life looked like *healing, salvation, miracles,* and *freedom*! These should flow from our lives too!

I find it fascinating that the below verse is sandwiched between verses about being *present* with the Lord. Look them up! There's a connection between our relationship to Him and our faith.

For we walk by faith, not by sight (2 Corinthians 5:7)

I believe this has been taken out of context and used as an excuse of why we don't see a move of God in our churches. I do not believe it was ever intended to mean such. We do walk by faith and not sight! I just happen to see this a little differently from some, I suppose. When I walk by faith, I *see* the sick person whole, I *see* the bound person free, I *see* the dry spiritual atmosphere becoming saturated with the tangible presence of God. And this faith that I have prompts me to *action* because faith without works is dead! Faith should produce two things: action on my part and results for what I'm believing for. **When faith reaches maturity, it becomes sight!** Jesus had perfect faith; consequently, He *saw* the supernatural manifest! Jesus had faith the blind man would see, and His faith became sight as the miracle was wrought!

*Then said Jesus unto him, "Except ye see signs and won-
ders, ye will not believe"* (John 4:48)

Jesus understood the need for the world to *see* something to draw them to salvation. Everywhere He went, He flowed in the supernatural. He did not get offended that the crowd needed to see something. In fact, Jesus' only problem seemed to be with the unbelievers who either rejected His miraculous work or denied His power altogether. I charge us to hold ourselves accountable to walk in the fullness of what God has for us and, if we are not there yet, shift accordingly. **Adjustment is the mark of maturity.** May we desire what He desires, things like people changing, sicknesses disappearing, demons fleeing, and freedom being released. These are wonderful indicators that the Kingdom has come! Let's kill every lie of excuse and step out in faith, on His word, so that we can *see* results and they can *see* Jesus! Everything Jesus did miraculously was through the power of the Holy Spirit. We have this same Spirit!

> *"Verily, verily, I say unto **you**, He that believeth on me, the works that I do shall he do also; and greater works than these shall he do…"* (John 14:12a)

Father, You have placed a high calling on each of us. You've instructed us what to do and how to do it. We repent of every excuse we've created for why we don't see Your Kingdom come. May our faith take feet and begin to move. Lord, Your first instruction to the disciples was to "Go." May that word be spoken over each one reading today! I pray for Your supernatural power to fill each one to overflowing. We love you, Lord, and pray all things in Jesus' authority! Amen.

Thursday Signs: What's This All About?

Part 1/2

Signs are not new for the Lord in relation to His people! Only nine chapters into the Bible and we find the first!

God's first covenant with man was marked with a sign.

"And I will establish My covenant with you; neither shall all flesh be cut off any more by the waters of a flood; neither shall there anymore be a flood to destroy the earth." And God said, "This is the **token** *of the covenant which I make between Me and you…I do set My bow in the cloud, and it shall be a* **token** *of a covenant between Me and the earth"* (Genesis 9:11-13)

According to *Strong's Concordance* H226,
the word for *token* is *owth*.[18]

The word *owth* is where we get our word *oath*. The meaning of *owth* is a signal, a flag, a beacon, a monument, evidence, a mark, a miracle, or a **sign**! When the Lord mentions *signs* in the Bible, we should take notice. They often relate to areas of covenant or promise! When Jesus was to be born, there was the *sign* in the sky of the star. I believe the Lord desires for us to gain understanding concerning His signs and the purpose they hold.

So let's dive right in!

And He (Jesus) said unto them, "Go ye into all the world, and preach the gospel to every creature. He that believeth and is baptized shall be saved; but he that believeth not shall be damned. And these **signs** **shall follow** *them that believe; 1.) In My name shall they cast out devils; 2.) They shall speak with new tongues; 3.) They shall take up serpents; and 4.) If they drink any deadly things, it shall not hurt them; 5.) They Shall lay hands on the sick, and they shall recover." So then after* the Lord had spoken unto them, He was received up into heaven, and sat on the right hand of God. And they went forth, and preached everywhere, the Lord working **with** them and **confirming the Word with SIGNS** following. Amen" *(Mark 16:15-20)*

Jesus operated in miracles. It's a fact. He went about healing and casting out demons. It's what He did. It's who He was and who He still is! We can like it or hate it, but the Word is clear on the subject. Immediately before ascending back to Heaven, He uttered a powerful declaration! Those last words are recorded in the Mark passage above. It is in these verses that I'd like to camp out today. These words have been misquoted, misrepresented, and misinterpreted. Often people in the church avoid or breeze past these verses due to the stigma that exists. Let's get this straight! Let's reason together, shall we? Jesus was about to ascend to Heaven, but first He wanted to say something, a final set of instructions, pretty important, right? I think what He said to that crowd should be a foundational point of discussion in our churches. Don't you? It was his last spoken words for goodness' sake. However, what we see too often in our church culture is the opposite. I'm here today to break that boundary wide open through the power of the Holy Spirit. After all, *He* is the teacher of the Word.

> *"Howbeit when he, the Spirit of Truth, is come, he will guide you into all truth"* (John 16:13)

The Holy Spirit within us is able to teach us the meaning of our opening scripture. However, it is through faith alone we receive from the Lord! So in believing that the Holy Spirit will speak, I type on! I've told you before, I have nothing to offer you of any lasting merit. We need to hear from Him. So let faith arise right now that you will hear from Him, and I know you will!

I look at the Mark passage like a vision/mission statement for the church. The vision is the overarching goal of the church: to go and preach the Gospel. It's *all* about the Gospel. The preaching of the cross sits at the center of the Kingdom of God. After the *go* vision is shared, Jesus goes into the details of what that looks like—He gives the nuts and bolts of it. He tells us in specific detail how we are to preach the Gospel. A vision statement is nothing without a tangible understanding of how to carry it out successfully, aka the mission. It's quite funny because the Lord gives us what we refer to as the *great co-mission*, right? *Co* means together. So He understands we need to work as a team to complete the mission, first with Him and secondly with one another. So in the mind of Jesus, the Gospel's work is enabled by casting out devils, speaking with new tongues, taking up serpents, being protected from threat, and healing the sick. Let's plunge further into each of these signs and destroy the lies so strategically implemented to keep us away from fulfilling our mission!

1) *Shall be Saved*—The word *saved* is from the Greek word *sozo G4982.*[19]

Many of us think it means "to be saved from Hell and go to Heaven," but its meaning is much richer! It actually translates: *safe, delivered, protected, healed, preserved, to do well,* or *to become whole.*

Ministering the Gospel with that definition looks different from what many of us are familiar with. No longer is preaching the Gospel simply stating, "Raise your hands for salvation and repeat a prayer. Bam! You're saved." No, now it becomes, "Come, give your life to Christ to receive safety, wholeness, healing, and deliverance. And best of all, receive restored relationship with the Father! Then go out and preach this Jesus to others!" Jesus' blood purchased far more than we receive, but it doesn't have to be that way. May we all be *saved* in the full sense of the word!

2) *And is Baptized*—John the Baptist summarizes this point so well in Matthew 3:11.

> *"I indeed baptize you with water for repentance, but the One who is coming after me is more powerful than I. I am not worthy to remove His sandals. He Himself will baptize you with the **Holy Spirit** and **Fire**."*

John makes a distinction between two different baptisms.

I can be ridiculed or hated for saying it, but I'll say it anyway. The Holy Spirit is greater than water. What do I mean? I am not belittling water baptism. I actually think it means *more* than we believe many times. It was never called a symbol biblically, but we portray it as such. The Word actually says in Romans 6:4 that we are buried with Christ through baptism so that we can be raised with Him in new life. So when my faith says, "When I go under the water, I die with Christ, and when I come out, I am raised with Him," I will be! *This*, my friend, is *water* baptism! It was never meant to be a photo-op; it was meant to seal salvation and kick the enemy out.

And then there's the second baptism that we *get to* partake in— the baptism of the Holy Spirit! We read in the book of Acts about a group of people set on fire by the filling of the Holy Spirit. They turned the world upside down. I would urge us all to ask to be filled not just once but daily!

"Be (being) filled with the Spirit" (Ephesians 5: 18b)

Power and Fire

This doesn't sound like a request to me; it sounds like a command! Then there's John 7:38 where we read, "He that believeth on Me, as the scripture hath said, out of his belly shall flow rivers of living water." This is the same picture of the Holy Spirit continually filling us! Let me interject something right here. The thief on the cross that would meet Jesus in Paradise did not get baptized with either baptism. Baptism does not save us. It is *only* the refusal of Jesus' sacrifice that one is not saved! "But he that believeth *not* shall be damned" (Mark 16:17). Being baptized strengthens our earthly walk and ministry and, of course, helps keep us on fire for God!

3) *Cast Out Devils*—First of all, everything done in the kingdom is completed in the name of Jesus. Remember that according to Strong's G3683, *name* translates as the *authority* and *character* of Jesus.

We walk in His authority over the enemy! That is the crux of the whole study: *Seated in the Clouds, Ruling on the Earth*! Yes, we are called to cast out devils...news flash! Jesus did it, we do it! I have had the privilege of praying with people and commanding the enemy to depart and watching his influence leave. I was praying over one girl; as a spirit of depression left her, her face lit up. She felt hope for the first time in years. The long-standing pain she had struggled with vanished. **I didn't even pray for the pain to leave, it just had to!** I didn't know she had been in pain. Some are taken with illnesses that are rooted in a foul spirit; aka a demon, a devil, and the only way for healing to come is to be rid of that influence. **We have to stop being so afraid of an enemy that we have been granted power over.** Demons are *real*, and they are *really* involved in our lives. Where there's strife, there's the enemy. Where there's hate, there's the enemy. Where there's fear, there's the enemy. Of course, I could go on and on. I could write a whole book on this one point. However, I'll summarize like Jesus did, "Cast out demons!" If they are in your home, if they are in your kids, if they are in your own heart or mind,

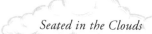
kick them out! Get mad and tell them to go! Some think Christians can't struggle with demons...wrongo! When Peter encouraged Jesus to bypass the cross, Jesus responded with, "Get behind me, Satan." **Satan's persuasion had entered Peter's mind and made its way to his mouth!** We are no different. In fact, wouldn't the enemy want us to think that he can't invade us so that he can keep doing his work undercover? Yikes! Remember he's a hider from the Garden. As a Christian, my spirit is saved and sealed with the Holy Spirit; however, I still have a body and a soul (mind, will, emotions). It is in these places that the enemy will invade through any open door he can such as depression, anger, bitterness, rejection, sickness, and the list goes on. He will invade as much as we will let him, I assure you! Kick him out today in the name and authority of Jesus! Cast out devils!

---

*Lord, You are looking for a people full of Your power and fire to turn this world upside down. We want to be **that** people. If Jesus needed the Holy Spirit to descend upon Him before He began ministry...if Peter needed the upper room experience before preaching, surely we do too! Touch the ones who are on fire with a deeper level of understanding of Your power, I pray! Those of us who have been filled but have grown lukewarm, light us on fire again! Those of us who have never encountered Your Holy Spirit-filling, today is the day! We ask to be filled! We ask in faith and await Your power to fall...even now! God, we anticipate Your move in our lives. In Jesus' name we ask for this power. Amen.*

Friday Signs: What's This All About?

Part 2/2

Continued from yesterday…

*"2.) They shall speak with new tongues; 3.) They shall take up serpents; and 4.) If they drink any deadly things, it shall not hurt them; 5.) They shall lay hands on the sick, and they shall recover." So then after the Lord had spoken unto them, He was received up into heaven, and sat on the right hand of God. And they went forth, and preached everywhere, the Lord working **with** them and **confirming the Word with signs** following. Amen."* (Mark 16:17b-20)

Let's continue to explore God's signs, shall we?

4) *Speak with New Tongues*—Yes, this is for today! The word *new* here comes from the Greek word, G2537 *kainos* and means "new especially in freshness."[20]

I love that! We need something fresh today, don't we? As a twelve-year-old, at an altar alone, I received the baptism of the Holy Spirit with the evidence of speaking in tongues or languages. Let me insert this thought: this is God's doing and God's design. If you have an issue with it, take it up with Him. I will submit to us that He does things in peculiar ways to challenge pride in us. Remember Him leading Naaman to dip seven times in the muddy Jordan to be healed? Remember Jesus spitting to make clay to heal someone's sight? He chose to fill us with His Spirit and give us an utterance to speak that makes us look foolish to the world. So what! I'm totally satisfied to be ridiculed by the world. It's when the church does the ridiculing of the work of the Holy Spirit that there's a big problem! As a matter of fact, Jesus Himself speaks quite sternly against anyone coming against the work of the Holy Spirit in Matthew 12:30-32: "He that is not with Me is against Me…The blasphemy (against) the (Holy) Ghost shall not be forgiven…Whosoever speaketh against the Holy Ghost, it shall not be forgiven him, neither in this world, neither in the (world) to come." These words rattle me to the core and serve as a warning for me to revere the work of the Holy Spirit. After all, the Holy Spirit *is* the Spirit of Jesus! Fear comes against His move because the enemy knows the power it brings. That foul spirit of fear masquerades as concern. Nope, fear *is* fear! But today, I speak in faith that there are two types of readers right now—those that *have been* filled with the Holy Spirit with tongues and those that *will be*! I urge you for your own good to seek the Lord in the quiet place and ask to be filled. Study this subject on your own. Do not take my word for it. Go to Acts! Go to Paul's epistles. Record the amount of times he enters a different church and asks the same question. "Have you received the Holy Spirit **since** you believed?" God is a rewarder of those who diligently seek Him. His gifts, even tongues, are always good and beneficial to the call. **It's not about you, it's about your call!** It's about being empowered with the might of the Holy Spirit, and **if you're afraid of Him, I can assure you, you aren't filled with Him.** He's a gentleman and won't enter a vessel that doesn't want Him. Be done with fear today and welcome the Lord fully!

5) *Take Up Serpents*—The enemy has had such a hay day with this one. He has religious zealots going around looking for poisonous snakes to handle. This goes against the Word that says the Lord has given us a sound mind.

As we have discussed, the enemy will do whatever he can to divert attention away from what the Scripture is *really* saying. The word for *serpent* here translates from Strong's G3789 *ophis* and means *Satan*. Hello! Satan was the serpent in the Garden of Eden.

He remains a slithering, sly, cunning creature. When he comes into our homes, our lives, and our relationships so subtly, we are called—actually commanded—to take him up and cast him out. Enough said! Get him out![21]

> *"But I fear…as the serpent beguiled Eve through his subtly, so your minds should be corrupted from the simplicity that is in Christ"* (2 Corinthians 11:3)

6) *If They Drink Anything Deadly*—The same God that did not call you to take up literal snakes did not call you to drink poison. This is rubbish! What God is promising, though, is protection to the believers.

Every one of these signs will only follow *believers*, right? So I took this verse literally for a loved one who took cancer treatment. I spoke over him that the deadly chemo, which he had to take into his body would not hurt him. I want to share with you, he sailed through chemo! Also, if there is a strategic attack assigned, or should I say *when there is*, the Lord promises protection to the believers. **Believer is not a title we carry; it is the lens through which we see every situation…the lens of Faith!** "For He shall give His angels charge over thee, to keep thee in all thy ways. They shall bear thee up in their hands, lest thou dash thy foot against a stone" (Psalm 91:11-12). Psalm 91, the whole chapter, is full of protection promises, but it all hinges on verse 1!

He that dwelleth in the secret place of the most High…

Without being a true believer and living in His presence, we *cannot* invoke His promises. It would be like a son that had moved out and abandoned his father but then came in demanding money. We have a part to play, a very important part, and these *signs* will follow them that **believe**!

7) *Lay Hands on the Sick*—Laying hands on the sick is a *sign* that shows up in a believer's life. What do you mean, April? Don't you mean the phrase, "and they'll recover," is

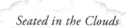
the sign? Why, yes, that is a sign too. But our text reads, "These *signs* shall follow them that believe…**they shall lay hands** on the sick and they recover."

If reading this creates an internal conflict, that's okay! Growth is good…painful but good! This is His Word, not mine. If I'm not one who desires to pray for the ill to be made well, can I be considered a true believer as it is defined above? I'm just posing a question. I have to check myself here as well. These words are hard to swallow, and I'm in the boat with you! I know that the *laying on of hands,* **action** must come before the, *they shall recover,* **result**; but I find myself so often chicken! Let's just be honest, shall we? I want them well, I know Jesus can, but I don't move beyond my fear. May we come to the point that our belief in His ability *and* desire to see them whole overcomes the fear the enemy places on us to not pray for them. Oh, that we would be the people of God unafraid and unashamed, believing *by His stripes* they will be *healed* but remembering that *it* comes through *our hands!* We know God is mighty, and we even believe He can do it through others. But I pray we will begin to launch out to *know* He will do it through us as well. Help us, Lord, cross the chicken line! You want them well.

If any of these signs are not following us, we need not be condemned or discouraged. We actually need to be quite encouraged because there is still time. However, let's not begin to chase after signs. Rather, let's chase after believing God! **God is worthy to be believed!** Then the signs will *follow* us! I understand that this word is challenging for many of us, me included, but the Word of the Lord is always accompanied by the ability of the Lord to fulfill it. Be filled with the Holy Spirit each day that your belief would grow and begin to attract signs like a magnet!

Father, I am humbled and challenged by Your Word today. According to Your scripture, I lack in areas of belief currently. I know this because all of Your signs are not chasing me. But I look to You and not to signs.

I know that as I cry out to You, You hear me and will fill me. Help my unbelief! Help our unbelief! Move our hearts to action. We will begin casting the enemy out of our lives and out of the lives of others! We want to be filled with Your Holy Spirit with the evidence You authored! May we be more aware of snakes that slither into our homes and promptly be rid of them. May we live under Your wings and protection as we stay close to You. And may we cross the chicken line and pray for the sick. Help us to be bolder to take authority over sickness and demons and kick them out, just like You did, Lord! May we challenge any area of our lives that does not match Yours. Help us in Jesus' name. Amen.

Saturday in Unity I Bow My Knee

22

From Him the whole body, joined and held together by every supporting ligament, grows and builds itself up in love, as each part does it work (Ephesians 4:16, NIV)

Some years ago, I began to notice that my right knee became uncomfortable upon kneeling. To further irritate the matter, my shoe got caught on carpet one day, and something popped in my knee. It grew more uncomfortable by the day. I remember not being able to freely walk while at work. At that time, I worked alongside surgeons, so I solicited the opinion of an orthopedist about my knee. Upon examination, he said it was likely a meniscus tear, and that does not resolve itself well at all. I thanked him and went about my day, believing God was my healer. Soon thereafter, I was with two of my prayer partners in worship and prayer together. One of the ladies requested prayer for her right knee. Something happened in me right before I started to pray for her. I said, "I'll agree for healing! Can y'all pray for my right knee too?" Then the third spoke up and asked for the same for her knee. We decided to sit down in a circle on the floor and pray for one another. Each of us had our two hands on the others' injured knees. We began speaking healing and life over one another's knees. We cried out fervently.

As I had become totally unaware of my own need and was crying out for my friends, something amazing began to occur. My right leg, the whole thing, began to shake under the power of God. I could feel something happening. I jumped to my feet and proclaimed, "I'm healed! I'm healed!" The first thing I did was to fall to my knees to see if that pain was gone...and it was! So I stood and fell again and again and again. Something so miraculous occurred that night for us. It was not just our physical healing that the Lord was administering, He brought a unity to us in prayer that unlocked His miracle power! Then we began to discuss what had happened. The above verse came to our minds. The Lord spoke and said, "Everything means something." We began to realize the reason our knees were the focus was because of the symbolic nature of how He was *joining us and holding us together by every supporting ligament* in unity *as* the body of Christ! It was so awesome, and I can bow my knee to this day without pain!

Lesson of the Day: Not getting results in prayer? Grab a partner, get in unity, and pray for them. Remember you reap when you sow. So sow into someone else in prayer and you will reap in your life!

Sunday Can You Hear Me Now? Why, Yes!

(photo and story approved for use by H. Sizemore)

Then the eyes of the blind shall be opened, and the ears of the deaf unstopped; then shall the lame man leap like a deer, and the tongue of the mute sing for joy. For the waters break forth in the wilderness, and streams in the desert (Isaiah 35:5-6, ESV)

Meet my dad and one of my favorite people! "I love this man" is an understatement. He loves his family, and he loves God. My dad is what you might call an adventurer. He continues to water ski to this day. For many years, he has raced dirt track race cars. This is a great place for him to share the light of the love of Jesus, but it is a loud place. My dad has struggled with hearing difficulty for many years and a few years ago purchased very costly hearing aids to help. And they did help.

One Sunday morning, our pastor was preaching on "Just Ask" from Matthew 7:7. My mom took my dad's hand and said, "Herb, I don't think you're going to have to wear those hearing aids anymore. I believe the Lord wants you healed of that." He agreed and quietly took his hearing aids out.

That night, after the pm service, my dad asked our pastor if he could give a testimony. Many of us were in the altar area, as we had been praying. He told us what had happened. When he took those hearing aids out, he began to hear more clearly. He had waited all day to tell anyone, testing out the hearing. But as he stood in the pulpit with tears streaming down his face, saying, "I can hear! I can hear!" I felt faith arising. This was the first I, as his daughter, was hearing of this too. It was awesome! After celebrating and praising the Lord, church was dismissed. I was lingering in the altar chatting with a friend when I heard my pastor calling my name. I turned, and he was standing with one of our special needs adult ladies. She came to him after service to have her ears healed too. She believed like a little child and took out her hearing aids. Before Pastor was done praying for her, she exclaimed, "I can hear! I can hear!" It was the sweetest thing ever.

Then the next Sunday morning, another lady stopped my pastor in the hall, and he spoke healing over her ears. Wouldn't you know it…healed! When my dad obeyed and took an action of faith, not only was he healed but other's faith also grew, and they were as well.

Lesson of the Day: Many are not healed *until* they take a step of faith. Remember Jesus said, "Rise, take up your bed, and walk," "Stretch out your hand." He often tied action to receiving. Then when God moves for you…TESTIFY! It will seal the deal, so to speak, and it may be just what someone else needs to hear.

Monday Rest: What Is It Good For? Absolutely Everything!

23

We've spent a lot of time thus far focusing the "ruling on the earth" aspect of our study. We pondered Adam and Eve's decision to sin, therefore forfeiting their rule on the earth over to the enemy. We've mentioned mighty men of God who displayed lives of surrender to God and victory over the enemy. Those men include: Joseph, Daniel, Joshua, Paul, Peter, John, and Jesus himself. But I believe there is a huge key to walking in authority on the earth that I'd like to bring awareness to. Today we will look deeper into the "seated in the clouds" portion of the study. And, boy, am I excited about it!

Many think that a spiritual warrior is the one who outshouts, outdances, and outprays the rest. People are looked at as *spiritual* if they are involved in a lot of ministries and able to juggle many kingdom activities. A few years back, the Lord revealed to me how absurd this was. I had a vision of a *warrior* with an intense look on their war-painted face. They were donned in full camo garb. Their posture was in constant fight position with every muscle in their body tensed, ready for action. Around them was blazing bullets and burning fires. Next, the Lord showed me a curly-haired little girl running through the daisies with not a care in the world. Then He asked me, "Which one is the enemy more afraid of?" My first instinct, which of course was carnal, was the military person. The Lord so gently brought an awareness that the child was far more frightening to the enemy. He began to peel back the layers of the vision and show me that the "warrior" was stressed, functioning in their own strength, and frustrated. But the little girl was completely at rest in her heart and mind because she was leaning on Christ. Peace was ruling in her life. She trusted so completely in her Father that she could easily say, "Devil, get out of here," and he'd have to go. All the strength that was being mustered by the militant was of their own merit. Yet the child rested fully in her Father's strength. Isn't that beautiful?

He who does not engage in the Lord's rest will eventually become powerless, unfruitful, and full of frustration. A true soldier of the Lord, one that is effective, lives in a posture of rest. However, to be explicitly clear, the Lord's rest does not entail inactivity! Like we've discussed before, the enemy always has a counterfeit to God's plan. The Lord provides rest, the enemy tempts with laziness. Many spend their lives on couches and Lazy-Boys, but they remain wearied and tired! Isn't this perplexing? The reason for this seemingly contradiction is that they are attempting to obtain rest, which only comes from God, through carnal means. One can sleep their days away and still be tired. Another could vacation fifty weeks out of the year and still need rejuvenation. What we need so desperately, especially in our rush-rush culture, is the Lord's rest.

There may be many reading right now that are thinking, "She's right. I really need to take that day a week to rest. I need to do better with keeping the Sabbath." But you know me by now! I will be going in a different direction. Remember, spiritual eyes must be enacted for this study! I believe there was one type of Sabbath in the Old Testament; however, there's a better kind of Sabbath mentioned in the New Testament! Many times physical principles in the Old Testament exist to point to spiritual principles for us today. I believe *Sabbath* is one of those principles that we neglect to fully understand.

> *And on the seventh day God finished His work that He had done, and He rested…So God blessed the seventh day and made it holy, because on it God rested from all His work that He had done in creation* (Genesis 2:2-3)

Above we hear the first mention of rest. God was the one doing the resting. After completing the amazing task of Creation, God did something very significant, He rested. I also find it quite intriguing that there is no mention of man taking one day off a week until Exodus, which was, of course, after sin entered. I would present to us that Adam and Eve, prior to sin, were in a perpetual state of constant rest. God *was* their rest! His very presence gave them rest. It was the *curse* that ushered in *working* by the *sweat of the brow*. Too many times we forget that the blood of Jesus restored our relationship with the Father to its original intention…*pre-sin*…*pre-curse*! This is fantastic news. I've not come with a message of, "Okay, everyone remember to do no physical work one day a week." I believe the Lord's message today goes deeper than *one* day of rest a week. He wants us to be restored to living in perpetual, continual rest through Jesus…who *is* our Sabbath!

> *"Come unto Me, all who labor and are heavy laden, and **I will give you rest**. Take My yoke upon you, and learn from Me, for I am gentle and lowly in heart, and you will **find rest** for your souls. For my yoke is easy, and My burden is light"* (Matthew 11:28-29)

When I read the above verses, the idea of one twenty-four-hour day is not what comes to my mind. That seems too narrow for the promise that I read. I believe Jesus offers us rest… rest that we can live in, rest that we should live in continually. It is these that makes the enemy tremble! Why? He knows their dependence is in their God and not in their works! Remember, God rested on the seventh day from His work. Seven represents completion. Christ came and fulfilled all the work necessary for us and then said, "It is finished (completed)." The cross and empty tomb moved us into the seventh day! Woohoo! Jesus went into Heaven, sat down, and rested from His work and we are, you guessed it, seated with Him! He rests, we rest!

I want to close today with a second vision the Lord gave me one night. I had to jump out of bed and draw what I saw. Its crude, but you'll get the gist. Two birds were flying. One was flapping for dear life. The moment it stopped flapping, it fell into a descent. The poor thing was winded, tired, and frustrated. Meanwhile, just a few yards over, there was the second bird. The wingspan was opened wide, and the bird just glided from side to side effortlessly. If a bird could smile, this one was smiling! You see the second bird had *found the wind!* The Lord spoke to me and said, "Stop flapping and simply find the wind." The Holy Spirit is the wind. Get in…nix that…*live* in His presence, and you will soar higher than ever before! And yes, you are totally free to shout for joy right now! I know I am! Praise God I've found the wind!

The wind bloweth where it listeth, and thou hearest the sound thereof, but canst not tell whence it cometh, and whither it goeth: so is every one that is born of the Spirit (John 3:8)

(sketch by A. Babb)

But they that wait upon the Lord shall renew their strength; they shall mount up with wings as eagles; they shall run, and not be weary; and they shall walk, and not faint (Isaiah 40:31)[24]

129

Oh, Lord, how magnificent are You in all Your ways. I'm amazed at how kind You are to pour into us during these days of devotion. You're reminding the sheep to rest beside still waters so that You can restore their souls. And, God, we respond! First, we repent of doing things in our own ability. We truly have been that militant individual, thinking that we are victorious, all the while, the enemy is laughing as we tire ourselves. God, we've leaned on our own strength too much. We all, like this first bird, have flapped until we couldn't flap anymore. But no more! God, may Your wind blow, and may we find it. Call us to the secret quiet place to be strengthened by You. We love You and are nothing without You. Call us up to higher places of rest today! In Jesus' name. Amen

Tuesday Walking it Out:
Humility and Unity

So we've talked a lot about being seated with Christ in heavenly places, but how do we actually do this? I've been pondering this lately. It is one thing to say be "seated in the clouds and rule on the earth," but it's another thing to live it out. We need to know how! Thankfully, the Holy Spirit is faithful to teach anyone willing to lean on Him for revelation. Let's believe that God is going to speak to us, and we are going to hear Him! Faith comes by hearing! Hearing comes by the Word. The Holy Spirit is the one who takes the Word and makes us to *hear* something. Holy Spirit, teach us practical application that we can begin to implement today! We want to do more than talk the talk; we want to know how to walk the walk!

As I began to meditate on how to be "seated with Christ," the word *unity* came to my mind. He has provided the opportunity for us to be unified together with Himself. It's because of His blood and His work alone that we can sit with Him. Be that as it may, we do have a role and a choice in the matter. Ultimately, our decision to stay close to Him brings about this unity. We must stay near to Him! Why do I say this?

*Beloved, **if** our heart condemn us not, **then** we have confidence toward God. And whatsoever we ask, we receive of Him, because we keep His commandments, and do those things that are pleasing in His sight. And this is the commandment that we should believe on the name of His Son Jesus Christ, and love one another, as He gave* *us commandment. And he that keepeth His commandment dwelleth in Him, and He in him. And hereby we know that He abideth in us, by the Spirit which he hath given us* (1 John 3:21-24)

My commentary goes a little like this: "If we have a clear conscience, we will be able to boldly run to God's throne. And because we live obedient to Him, we can ask what we want and receive it. The reason for this is that our wants will be in line with His will as we walk in this obedience to Him. That obedience being 1) *believing* on Him and 2) *loving* people. When we live like this, we are demonstrating that we are united with God. All this is accomplished by His Spirit!"

Verse 21 reads, *"If our heart does not condemn us, we have boldness (or confidence) toward God."* This is a doctrine that, I feel, we leave unanswered too often. We tell people, "You're seated with Christ! You are *in* Christ Jesus! Ask what you will, and it'll be done unto you." But we rarely mention the connection with our *behavior* and our *believing*. A sinning heart is a heart that will condemn itself...every time! It can't help it. Consequently, lifestyle affects our ability to boldly approach the throne of grace to make our petition known to God. This is not because God needs us to be *good* to receive, He doesn't! He needs us to have *faith* to receive. But according to the above verse, our heart cannot boldly approach God in this faith without walking in His ways. I believe the solution for us is found in verse 24, "He that keepeth His commandment dwelleth in Him, and He in him." Is this not the most beautiful way to describe unity with Jesus, He in us and us in Him? And what is His commandment? I'm glad you asked! In wonderful simplicity, verse 23 mentions 1) *believe on the Jesus Christ* and 2) *love one another*! That's right! I'm not here to bring back the law. I don't want us in bondage to a million dos and don'ts! But God enables us to obey as we stay close. In that place, there is a beautiful balance of walking in obedience to the command to *believe God* and *love people* that helps us realize our unity with Jesus![25]

I believe so much is about perspective! We *are* seated with Christ in Heavenly places (Ephesians 2:6). That work was done by God himself.

> *But God, who is rich in mercy, for His great love where-*
> *with He loved us, even when we were dead in sins, hath*
> *quickened us together with Christ, (by grace ye are saved ;)*
> *And hath **raised** us up together, and **made** us sit together*
> *in heavenly places in Christ Jesus* (Ephesians 2:4-6)

Your mission is not to work your way up a ladder to be able to sit with Jesus. Remember you are *already* sitting there…now! Living in obedience to the Lord opens our eyes to this reality where we are able to boldly approach Him and ask what we will. We will live with a heart that does not condemn us! The idea of being unified with Jesus boils down to one word: humility! I believe humility is the glue that holds me close to Jesus. It identifies me with Him, to others, to the Father, and to the enemy. The commandment of the Lord requires humility to live out. Remember our two mandates of believing and loving? Believing the Lord takes humility. We must know that on our own we're nothing and are in desperate need of Him. The humble person cannot be stopped from getting on their knees because they know their utter dependence on the Lord! God loves this! **Pride never take a knee!** Hmmm…Ouch! Lord, convict and cleanse us of all prideful attitudes we've lived with far too long! Loving others takes humility. There is a death to self that must occur as we sacrifice our desires for theirs.

I believe our greatest calling is godly humility! I am not condoning being a floor mat, or even a wimp! However, I am calling us **to stand in the courage it takes to bow down low**. And no, that is not an oxymoron!

The way up is always down!

Jesus was born in a barn and placed in a slop trough surrounded by animals. He grew up in a Jewish family lacking any notoriety. He hung out with fishermen, tax collectors, and sinners. He submitted to a wild-haired, bug-eating wilderness man and was dunked in a dirty river. He washed feet, prayed alone, fed others, and by choice, died in the greatest act of humility that would ever be undertaken! Wouldn't a life unified with Jesus look like Jesus' life?

Living in humility will open our eyes to the unity God has awarded us in Heaven with Christ. Isn't this awesome? God has placed us in unity with Jesus, but He didn't leave us out of the equation. Our obedience makes our heart to see clearly the surrounding clouds and the closeness of Jesus. So the practical, tangible one-step program for being "seated with Christ" is to—get a notebook and a pen, write it down, here it is, I don't want you to miss it—*walk humbly*! That's it! When in doubt, respond with humility! When hurt by others, respond with humility! When pride is pressing in hard, respond with humility! The lower you go, the higher you soar! Let's live low just like our Jesus did so that we can be raised with Him to rule and reign!

---

*Father, we **are** seated right beside you with Christ right now! If we are a blood-bought child of God, we are there! But we want to be empowered by a life of obedience to live like it! I pray that you would impart a holy, set-apart, humility in each of our hearts. We know the process of death to self is painful, but we want it anyway! God, we crucify our flesh by making decisions to regard others better than ourselves. We want to be identified with Jesus in every way. Holy Spirit, enable us with the strength only you can provide to pull this off! **We cannot grit our teeth and be humble. That is pride trying to enable humility in us. How absurd!** Lord, in full dependence on You, we ask for help. Help us believe You and love others. We do not want our hearts to condemn us ever again. In Jesus' name we ask all things. Amen.*

Wednesday Reason or Faith:
The Choice is Yours

Part 1/2

As we rapidly approach the conclusion of this study, I've asked the Lord what He has in mind for these last three days. And as usual, He gave me instruction for just today. The greatest moments in my Christian walk occurred when I was forced to rely solely on God to tell me what to do next. These moments breed the supernatural. This is walking by faith and not by sight. Manna came down to provide for that day alone. God still offers us *daily bread*, aka His Word! I remember preparing for this study and numbering 1 to 30 on a sheet of paper with "Seated in the Clouds, Ruling on the Earth" written at the top. Immediately, I heard the Lord say, "What are you doing, child?" "Well, Lord, I'm planning out this study." Then I dropped the pen as I heard Him say, "Trust me each day to speak through you what I want to be said. You can come up with an agenda, but wouldn't you rather be sourced by my Spirit each day with fresh revelation?" I crumpled the paper and went on about my day. My *sight* wanted to know ahead of time what the study would hold, but that was not walking by *faith*. Each night, I sat down at the computer and waited quietly. I learned to pray this prayer, "Holy Spirit, You're in me. I give You this mind, this heart, and these fingers to type what You want to say to the people." And then an idea, a picture, a scripture would come to my mind; and I would begin typing. I believe these are powerful keys to our hearing from God: wait quietly, believe God is going to speak, and listen. I am not saying any of this to draw attention to myself because if you look closely at me, you will see much to be desired! I am sharing this to show you a tangible example of how to trust God and not your own intellect, reasoning, or mental capacity.

From the beginning, a war has been waged between the carnal and the spiritual part of us. Satan used reasoning to trick Eve: "Has God (really) said…?" It is still a sharp weapon in his arsenal. I know individuals who served God wholeheartedly during their young adult life; however, when they grew up and became *educated*, they turned away from God. We see so many *intellectuals* of our day that know a lot but know nothing of real importance. A person can have the knowledge and skill set to do brain surgery but be unaware of how to unclutter their own mind. Another can have the intellect to trade stocks and become a millionaire but be spiritually bankrupt! I want to encourage us today to challenge ourselves concerning this. Are we leaning on the Lord's wisdom or our own intellect? As I learn more about the things of God, and I have a long way to go, I realize how heavily we lean on our intellect, learning, and human reasoning.

We even encounter this in church circles. Sister Sally asks for prayer for cancer, "It's bad," she says, "stage four," with a sunken countenance on her face. Then someone responds with, "Oh, Sally, I'm *so* sorry. That's *terrible* news. How far has it spread? Maybe you should go to the Mayo Clinic?" Yada, yada, yada and other unhelpful things uttered. My point is simple. Do we believe God's Word or not? It is time to be honest with ourselves and ask these hard questions! I do not celebrate when I hear of these diagnoses, I can assure you of that! I recently had a wonderful grandfather pass of cancer. It was awful and *not* of God. But if we are called to rule on the earth over sicknesses like Jesus did, we must believe and live by Isaiah 53:4-5.

> *Surely He took up our pain and bore our suffering, yet we considered Him punished by God, stricken by Him, and afflicted. But He was pierced for our transgressions, He was crushed for our iniquities; the punishment that brought us peace was on Him, and **by His wounds we are healed**.*

Is it His will to heal some of the diseased and let others suffer? Intellect will say, "Look, we all have to die sometime." But faith says, "We all have to die, but not at the hand of the enemy's diseases!" Yes, **healing is for all according to the Word and according to His wounds!** Think about it. If it was not His will to heal someone, wouldn't we be in disobedience to pray healing over them? Goodness, they shouldn't take any medicine to heal them either if it's God's will for them to be sick, right? Of course, that train of *thought* is rubbish and actually demonic. We must never deny the Word because circumstances do not line up. *Spoiler alert: Circumstances can tell lies!*

Father, we lean in, even now, to incline our ear to hear from You! We state our desire to walk by faith and by Your voice! We repent of our tendency to lean on our mental intellect to guide our lives. We take authority over our carnal minds and the lies that are fed into it, and we receive the mind of Christ! Father, we love You and thank You for gently guiding us onto the path of faith! In Jesus' name we pray all prayers. Amen.

Thursday Reason or Faith: The Choice Is Yours

Part 2/2

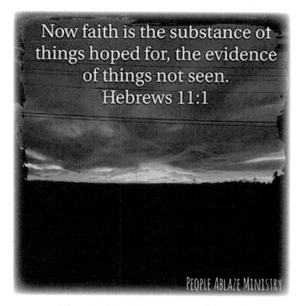

Now faith is the substance of things hoped for, the evidence of things not seen. Hebrews 11:1

PEOPLE ABLAZE MINISTRY

(photo by Kim Ray, approved for use)

I pray we are coming to an understanding that faith and intellect oftentimes do not mix well. If your intellect, which is factual-based, says something is true, then why do you need faith to believe it? Intellect is like vinegar that is sour and pungent, and faith is the oil that flows from deep within. Faith says, "It looks grim, it sounds grim, it smells grim, it feels grim, it even tastes grim, but I believe goodness is coming forth!" **Faith doesn't ignore or pretend the issue isn't present; it just refuses its right to stay that way!**

On the other hand, intellect says, "People I know with that diagnosis died…Let's not get our hopes up…What are my chances, Doctor?" and other *doubtful,* but *factual stuff!* Intellect speaks in facts, and we are in love with the facts.

They make us comfortable as they imprison us.

We want the stats, we want the odds, we crave knowledge. Our minds are so full of knowledge that our head outweighs our bodies! We live in an age where nothing is unknown. Think about it! In half a second, I can Google, well, anything! Don't misunderstand me, I appreciate the ability to Google the weather in Timbuktu, if I'm interested. However, I believe the church has too often fallen prey to the same trick Eve did! Let's go to Scripture for more clarity!

*For the weapons of our warfare are not **carnal**, but mighty through God to the pulling down of strong holds; Casting down imaginations, and every high thing that exalteth itself against the knowledge of God, and bringing into captivity every thought to the obedience of Christ (2 Corinthians 10:4-5)*

Greek School: 2 Corinthians 10:4-5 Strong's Concordance References			
Word	Greek Word	Strong's Number	Meaning
Weapon	Hoplon	G3696	*Offensive* tool used for offensive warfare
Warfare	Strateua	G4752	Apostolic (to be sent out, aka us!) career hardships and dangers
Carnal	Sarkikos	G4555	Fleshly, bodily, (relating to the five senses), temporal
Pulling Down/Casting Down	Kathairesis	G2506	Demolition, obliteration, extinction, annihilation, to lower, to destroy
Stronghold	Ochuroma	G3794	Fortified by holding safely (so a stronghold makes us feel safe as it imprisons us!)
Imaginations	Logismos	G3053	Computation, reasoning, conceit, though
Knowledge	Gnosis	G1108	The act of knowing (in this verse it relates to knowledge of Christ)
Obedience	Hupakoe	G5218	Attentive hearkening, compliance, or submission

26

139

Before I received revelation on these verses, I was unaware of the danger of trying to mix faith with logic to accomplish things in the kingdom. I am not imposing that reason is all bad. It has its place in our lives. We see a hot stove, and logically we do not touch it. We use reason to balance our checkbooks, complete our daily tasks, and slam on the breaks when a deer crosses our path. Intellect isn't evil; it's just a tool for the *natural realm*. Faith is for the *spiritual realm*. I wouldn't use an automotive tool in surgery or a surgical instrument to repair an engine. It's when we try to apply logic to spiritual matters that there's a problem. The danger of allowing this process of thought into our faith walk is found in the very definition of the word.

Reasoning: The process of forming conclusions, judgments, or inferences from **facts**[27]

As discussed in prior days, we are called to *go and preach the Gospel*. "Cast out devils, speak with new tongues, take up spiritual serpents, and lay hands on the sick" (Mark 16:17-8). Reason will not allow these activities to be done…*ever*! Reason says, "Someone else will share the Gospel. You're not called to do that. God knows you have a job, husband, and five kids. Surely, He doesn't expect that of you." Reason mocks the Word of God and says, "Cast out devils, speak with new tongues. Huh! What's all this **nonsense** (lacking agreement with the senses, did you catch that)! I mean let's be **reasonable**! That's **crazy**! You just need to read the Bible and pray, no need to do anything more than that. **Learn** more Bible verses, yes, that's all you need to do. The fanatics that do all that stuff just don't **know** their Bibles. They need to learn more." I've used bold lettering to alert you to keywords that you will hear from the mouth of reason, but you need to speak **BOLD** words back to the enemy! The voice of reason will never call you to act but to keep filling your head with knowledge. Everything God calls us to do in faith will be challenged by the strongholds of logic, computation, and reason. Call it what you will, but it is the primary language of Hell itself! Remember Satan's first uttered words were, "Has God (really) said?" Don't fall for it. The thoughts stopping you from moving forward in the call are not your thoughts. The comfortable prison wall of logic must come down in Jesus' name!

> It's time to do some pulling down of strongholds, casting down of imaginations, and bringing into prison those very thoughts that have imprisoned you!

I declare and prophesy over you, it is the season of the turnaround. It is a season of action and activity for the kingdom. It's time to move and advance His will on the earth! Do something! We've been equipped, we've learned His word, now it's time to impart something to others. May every voice in your head, which is not God's, be exposed. Sometimes we need to walk around our own mind and say, "Devil, you don't speak here!" **Faith is our substance, and we *will* get our *hopes* up…*high*!** Our Lord has made promises, and they will outweigh what we see with our eyes from this point on! We will walk by faith!!

Father, I hear You declaring freedom over Your people today! You are our Deliverer. Our role is to believe, and Your role is the performance portion. We will believe the report of the Lord! No longer will we be swayed by facts! God, Your truth overrules facts and will change the facts as we believe. Empower us now, Holy Spirit, to grow in our faith. May we see that faith and logic are vinegar and oil in our soul! They cannot mix. Logic has no place in our spiritual walk. God, do as only You can do and breathe on this devotion today and awaken it to every listening heart. We want Your fresh manna today. We will learn to wait upon You each day for direction for that day alone. Separate us from our addiction to our lists, logic, facts, and reasoning. We surrender our minds to You today. Use us mightily for Your kingdom, we pray. In Jesus' name we pray. Amen.

Friday Let's Go!

28

In 2015, as I lay in bed praying, the Lord showed me the words: "Seated in the Clouds, Ruling on the Earth." I never imagined what a fulfilling adventure He was leading me to! Today the message I bring is a simple one:

It's your time to fly!

The Lord has given clear direction for this last day. We have learned what it means to be *seated with Christ in heavenly places.* God encouraged us to rest in Christ and, by doing so, receive strength for the journey. He also demonstrated through Scripture what a victorious life looks like, here on earth. We were reminded that the work of Jesus purchased our freedom from the enemy. Through His name we are to walk in that freedom and authority each and every day. We were exhorted to follow His *command* to be filled with His Spirit, heal the sick, cast out devils, speak with new tongues, take up spiritual serpents, and live in His protection.

So now we find ourselves with all this biblical knowledge of our call; what are we going to do about it? I hear the Lord say, "Will you be a doer or just a hearer of My Word?" He is challenging us all, myself included, to take action. A rocket on a launching pad is full of potential but accomplishes nothing just sitting there. He is God, and He changes not! His command to the first disciples was the same command He gives us today, "Go!"

He said unto them, "Go into all the world and preach
the gospel to the whole creation" (Mark 16:15)

I would be remiss to teach these biblical truths to you and not urge you to act upon them. I believe there are those reading that are called to increase the *volume* of their outward witness. Others are called to jump into the unknown by faith of what God has for them. Some have been waiting to minister *until* something else happens or they learn more or they improve on themselves. The Lord says "until" is a lie from the enemy that will forever keep you from your destiny. God knows exactly where you are and who you are. He knows your weaknesses and flaws, and He still calls you to go! He is aware of the insecurity, yet He still calls you to go! Write the book, invite her/him to church, start the prayer meeting, post that video of encouragement. Do something! Leave a legacy for the Kingdom of Christ! You will learn along the way, believe me on that one! But you must start somewhere, and the first step is usually trembling all the way. But isn't that the way of faith, trembling all the way? If we're not a bit unsure and shaken, we probably are just *doing it* in ourselves, and that is *not* what we want to do.

Remember when I shared that I wanted to plot out all thirty days of what I would write about in this devotion but that the Holy Spirit did not give me peace about that? Instead, He had me quietly listen and write what I heard each day. This required more faith of me than having an agenda typed up ahead of time. **When more faith is required to complete a task, there's more room for miracles to**

flow. Think about it. He says, "Pray for the sick." Who's ever *ready* for that? No one is. That's why His power can flow, because we have none in that area. I do not need His power to flow to brush my teeth; I can do it quite well on my own. It is routine, mundane, and pretty boring honestly (I do it anyway just in case you were wondering). But I need the Holy Spirit's power to speak deliverance over someone or to preach the Gospel. When I launch out in faith and do these things, the supernatural has just come into the natural. You have not lived until you have had no idea what to do without Him.

I realize that today's message is simple. But that's how I'm being led to write. No deep doctrinal revelations are needed today. God simply says, "Go!" He also says that each person knows exactly what their "go" looks like. It's what you think about, dream about, but have been too afraid to step out for in His kingdom. He doesn't call us to do things we hate. He's a good Father. *He* puts *His* desires in us and then calls us to perform them through *His* anointing. When He gives us these desires, He usually does not endow us with self-confidence in these areas purposefully! Abraham was called to be the father of a nation but was ninety and childless. He had to have God's help. Moses was called to speak on behalf of the entire nation of Israel but had a stuttering problem. He had to have God's help. We are called to be a voice in this generation for the Lord. We have to have God's help.

I can hear some of you now thinking to yourselves, "But, April, I've never felt His power move upon me like you describe. How could I step out?" I have an answer for you! You are looking at it wrong, my friend! I never felt His power *until* I stepped out. We want it the other way, but He requires us to step out in faith, and then His power meets us! Don't worry, just go. I mean, here I am working on a book. I understand being scared! I have no idea what I'm doing, but I'm doing it anyway! Come and join me. It's a great, thrilling, fun, and exciting journey, one of which you'll never regret taking!

Father, I'm in awe that this day is really here. You have been so kind to pour out revelation each day, and we thank You. All glory and honor to

You alone for this compiled work. I pray people will be forever changed, able to sit with You in Heaven and rule over their enemy on the earth. May the Great co-mission be burned into our hearts. May our love for them outweigh our fear of them so that we can reach them. Help us preach the good news in its entirety in Jesus' name. We love You, Lord. Amen.

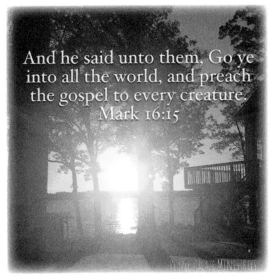

(photo by A. Babb)

April is available for speaking engagements.

Please contact her via email @ PeopleAblaze@gmail.com

Reference

1 Strong, James. "Creeping Thing." *Strong's Expanded Exhaustive Concordance of the Bible.* Nashville: Thomas Nelson, 2009. Print.

2 *(photoviaPixabay, https://pixabay.com/en/ board-slate-blackboardfont-939244/)*

3 *(photoviaPixabay, https://pixabay.com/en/ banner-header-attentioncaution-1165975/)*

4 * bibleresearch.info

5 Strong, James. "Officer." *Strong's Expanded Exhaustive Concordance of the Bible.* Nashville: Thomas Nelson, 2009. Print.

6 *(photoviaPixabay, https://pixabay.com/en/lion-zoo-cage-624457/)*

7 *(photoviaPixabay, https://pixabay.com/en/ clouds-sky-boot-sea-waterwaves-808748/)*

8 *(photoviaPixabay, https://pixabay.com/en/ girl-field-runningoutside-window-1666678/)*

9 *(photoviaPixabay, https://pixabay.com/en/ woman-girl-freedomhappy-sun-591576/)*

10 *(photoviaPixabay, https://pixabay.com/en/ king-crown-historyromania-1304612/)*

11 *(photoviaPixabay, https://pixabay.com/en/ king-crown-historyromania-1304612/)*

12 Authority. (n.d.). *Merriam-Webster's* online dictionary (11th ed.)Retrieved from http:www. merriam-webster.com/dictionary/authority

13 Strong, James. "Authority." *Strong's Expanded Exhaustive Concordance of the Bible*. Nashville: Thomas Nelson, 2009. Print. Strong, James. "Name." *Strong's Expanded Exhaustive Concordance of the Bible. Nashville: Thomas Nelson, 2009. Print.*

15 Supernatural. (n.d.). *Merriam-Webster's* online dictionary (11thed.) Retrieved from http:www.merriam-webster.com/dictionary/supernatural

16 *(photoviaPixabay, https://pixabay.com/en/book-old-clouds-treebirds-bank-863418/)*

17 *(photoviaPixabay, https://pixabay.com/en/rainbow-canim-lakebritish-columbia-183538/)*

18 Strong, James. "Token." *Strong's Expanded Exhaustive Concordance of the Bible*. Nashville: Thomas Nelson, 2009. Print.

19 Strong, James. "Saved." *Strong's Expanded Exhaustive Concordance of the Bible*. Nashville: Thomas Nelson, 2009. Print.

20 Strong, James. "New." *Strong's Expanded Exhaustive Concordance of the Bible*. Nashville: Thomas Nelson, 2009. Print.

21 Strong, James. "Serpent." *Strong's Expanded Exhaustive Concordance of the Bible*. Nashville: Thomas Nelson, 2009. Print.

22 *(photoviaPixabay, https://pixabay.com/en/cross-sunsetsilhouette-human-106416/)*

23 *(photoviaPixabay, https://pixabay.com/en/fence-road-landscapecountryside-996620/)*

24 *(photoviaPixabay, https://pixabay.com/en/prairie-steppes-mountains-1025229/)*

25 *(photoviaPixabay, https://pixabay.com/en/rock-heart-love-hardstone-pebble-80074/)*

26 Strong, James. "Weapon, Warfare, Carnal, Pulling Down, Stronghold, Imaginations, Knowledge, Obedience." *Strong's Expanded Exhaustive Concordance of the Bible*. Nashville: Thomas Nelson, 2009. Print.

27 http://www.dictionary.com/browse/logic?s=t

28 *(photoviaPixabay, https://pixabay.com/en/rocket-launch-rockettake-off-nasa-67643/)*

About the Author

April Babb is a wife, a mother of five, a registered nurse, an ordained preacher, and a ministry partner with her husband, Paul. But above all, she is on fire for the Lord and for bringing His kingdom to the earth! Together with Paul, she enjoys: preaching, writing, teaching, counseling, leading prayer, or just fishing. Currently, they are involved in various ministries in their community. These include Christian Heritage Church Prayer Team, Pastoral Care Partners, Facebook Ministry Community, and raising their wonderful children—the greatest ministry of all. They also host a Christian talk show every Monday called *Morning Manna: Bringing Joy to the Listener*. Some of her other passions include: leading worship, painting, sketching, mentoring other women, and releasing videos of encouragement each week. She has been privileged to see many healed, delivered, and encouraged by the power of the Holy Spirit.

People Ablaze Ministry, aka Paul & April Ministry, was birthed out of a deep-seated desire to see people set aflame with the Holy Spirit's power and fire. Their mission is: "Joining with Others to Bring Revival."

CPSIA information can be obtained
at www.ICGtesting.com
Printed in the USA
FSOW03n0520041117
40638FS

WHEN PEACE, LIKE A RIVER, ATTENDETH
MY WAY, WHEN SORROWS LIKE SEA
BILLOWS ROLL; WHATEVER MY LOT,
THOU HAS TAUGHT ME TO SAY,

*"It is well,
it is well
with my soul."*

~ SUNDAY CLASSES MORNINGS & THE REST OF OUR WEEK ~

J.O.Y. (Just Older Youth) Sunday School Class meets Sunday Morning at 10:00am in classroom 209! Come join us **as we continue to grow in God's Word** using New Life's "A Spiritual Adventure in Learning" Curriculum. **We also take up prayer requests**. We would love for you to come join us and be a part!

Bible Basics - meets **Sunday mornings 10^{am}** - Praise God - this class has grown so much that it has moved to the Fellowship Hall. Everyone is invited and if you have questions, bring those with you too! Hope to see you soon ~ *Sister Edna Murdaugh* .

Spiritual Freedom Network Classes Sunday Morn - - 10^{am} ~ *Dr. Fent, Pastor ~ Jason Hicks & ~ Donna Roberts*

Ushers/Greeters Ministry: Wanted! Wanted! Wanted!
"Committed" & **"Dedicated"** individuals willing to SERVE on the Team!
Our Meetings: We meet every 2nd Sunday, 9:30^{am}. You are welcomed to attend if you are interested in joining our Ministry Team ....Please see ~ *Brother Terry or Sister Sabrina* ~
No PM Service on Sundays changes to be announced.
!st Tuesday of everyMonth - Join us in the Sanctuary for a time of corporate Prayer
Tuesday Prayer 7:00^{pm} in the sanctuary. The *1st Tuesday of every month at 7pm til 8pm* - - - we come together corporately before the LORD in Praise , Prayer &Worship!!! Hope to see you there!

~ WEDNESDAY NIGHT CLASSES ~
Wednesday Bible Classics Study- 7^{pm} Room 209 - ~ *Pastor Bill George*
Wednesday Discipleship Class - 7^{pm} Room 208 ~ *Tom Belliveau*
Wednesday SINGLES CLASSES - Mans's Word VS. the Commandments of GOD Study - 7^{pm} Meet us in Room #207 ~ *Dot Sease*
Wednesday Praise & Worship Class - 8^{pm} Sanctuary ~ *Zack Hawkins*
3rd Thursday of each Month - 50+ Young At Heart Fellowship Dinner - held every 3rd Thursday at 6:30^{pm}. . Look for the Planning to Attend & Menu Sign-Up Sheets in the foyer. **Come join us!** "Be there, or be Square!" ~*Evangelist TD & Sis Rose Shaffer*

~ Ministry of Music ~
Friday 6th 7PM & Saturday 7th - Revival Fire World Outreach at Williston High School Stadium ~ Tina Camp ~ Praise & Worship led by Zack Hawkins ~
Saturday, March 27th & 28th - *Save the Date* - Leadership Workshop - *Obedience Creates Encounter* - Plan to join us ~ *Zack Hawkins*

Ministry Meetings
Saturday Life Builders & Ladies Ministry next quarterly meeting will be at **9:30^{am} May 2nd, 2020**.
Join us. **Life Bulider's** *Parents please do not release your children outside to play on the equipment - construction is not yet finished!* Safety measures are still being implemented.

1st March Printing

© 2018 Broadman Church Supplies Nashville, TN
Printed in the USA.

BR⊕ADMAN
CHURCH SUPPLIES

Hymn: It Is Well
With My Soul
634337889016